A PICTORIAL HISTORY OF THE SS

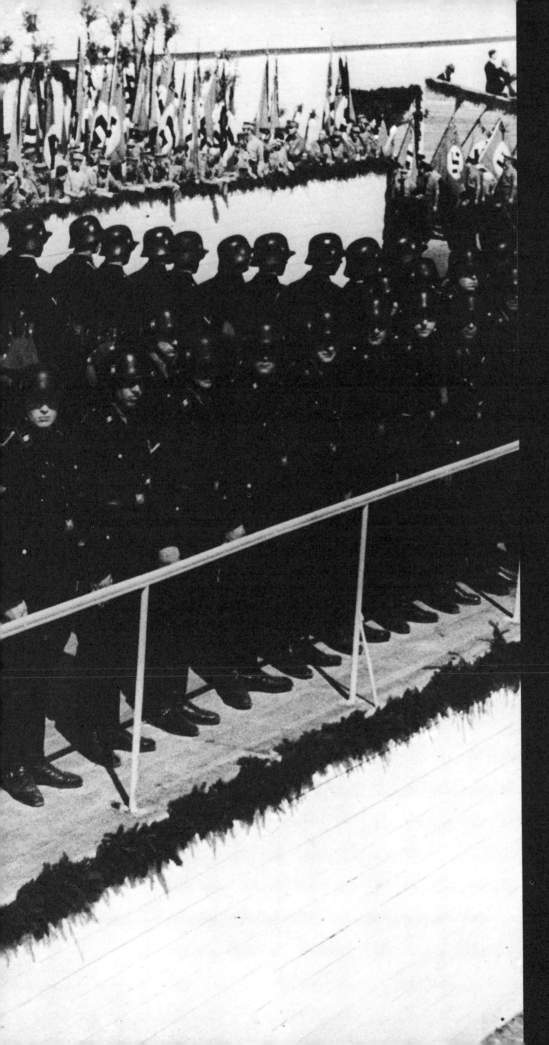

A PICTORIAL HISTORY OF THE SS

1923-1945

Andrew Mollo

Introduction by
Hugh Trevor-Roper

STEIN AND DAY
Publishers
New York

(Frontispiece) SS guards surround the
speaker's podium at the huge rally
held at the Tempelhof field on 1 May
1934

First published in the United States of America, 1977
Copyright © 1976 by Andrew Mollo
All rights reserved
Printed in the United States of America
Stein and Day/*Publishers*/Scarborough House,
Briarcliff Manor, N. Y. 10510

Library of Congress Cataloging in Publication Data
Mollo, Andrew.
    A pictorial history of the S.S.

    Bibliography: p. 192
    Includes index.
    1.   Nationalsozialistische Deutsche Arbeit-Partei.
Schutzstaffel–Pictorial works.   I.   Title.
DD253.6.M64   354'.43'0074   76-49044
ISBN 0-8128-2174-0

CONTENTS

PREFACE

Whilst the concentration camps have replaced Dante's inferno as the twentieth century vision of hell, the Waffen-SS has succeeded in elevating itself to the martial hall of fame alongside Attila's hordes, Rome's legions, and Napoleon's Old Guard, and the word Gestapo is still synonymous with suppression. But little attention has been paid to the political branch of the SS – the mainly part-time Allgemeine or General SS – and yet its 200,000 members were the grass roots of the SS, and its foundation. Without it there would have been no SS concentration camps, no Security Service (SD), and no Waffen-SS. However hard the Waffen-SS apologists argue to the contrary all these offshoots grew from the same SS tree.

Of all the many books written about the SS, only a handful have dealt with the SS as a whole. The pictorial histories concentrate exclusively on the Waffen-SS, so what better way to redress this imbalance than by producing the first pictorial history of the whole SS? Considerable thought was given to the organisation of the photographs, and it was finally decided to arrange them chronologically, rather than in groups dealing with a particular aspect. In this way one gets a much better idea of how the SS expanded – slowly at first – before emerging as the most powerful organisation of the Third Reich. This power is reflected in the development of the SS uniform, which at first was almost indistinguishable from the rather plebeian one of the SA, but which soon became elegant enough for the aristocrats, which the SS was trying to attract into its ranks.

In my opinion a historial photograph is only as valuable as the information that accompanies it, and so great care has been taken to identify as many of the personalities and localities as possible. One must also remember that photographs have always been, and still are, subject to censorship and distortion (see for example 11), and so each has been carefully checked, and not even original captions have been taken at their face value. Unlike many pictorial histories, photographs have not been juggled to fit the text, nor have they been captioned to suit the narrative. It is surprising how the same photograph is used in one book to illustrate the beastliness of the Spanish Nationalists during the Spanish Civil War, and German atrocities in Poland in another. Heaps of corpses piled in the streets of Dresden after the Allied air raid become victims of German atrocities in Russia and so on. It is obvious that the same standards of scholarship should be applied to illustrated books as to any other historical publication.

A sure knowledge of SS uniform enables one accurately to caption many photographs for the first time. SS rank badges were conveniently silver on black and they show up even in the murkiest of photographs. Once one has established a person's rank and identified the other insignia on his uniform, one is half way to identifying the person. The date of introduction of items of uniform or insignia also gives a clue to the date on which the photograph was taken.

The photographs reproduced here – many for the first time – come in the main from photographic agencies, archives, and private collections in Europe and the American continent, and I would like to thank the directors and their staffs and the collectors for their help in providing the photographs. In particular I would like to thank Thomas W. Pooler for allowing me to reproduce photographs of the Himmler documents in his possession, Michael Stevens of Macdonald and Jane's for his support and advice during the preparation of this book, and Hugh Trevor-Roper for writing the introduction.

Andrew Mollo London May 1976

INTRODUCTION

The SS was the peculiar institution of Nazism. It was the engine of terror without which Nazism would not have been itself and Hitler might never have solidified his power. It was also the ideological *corps d'élite* without which he could never have pursued his distinctive aims or realised his grim philosophy.

Every revolution needs such an instrument. Had Hitler not possessed it, he would have fallen into dependence on the established social forces, and the established political parties, of Germany. That, of course, is what the established politicians hoped to see. At one time they thought that their hopes were being fulfilled. They were sadly mistaken. Thanks to the SS, Hitler, the revolutionary genius who came to power in a correct, constitutional manner, was able to remain a permanent revolutionary, and his revolution maintained its momentum to the end. It was not a revolution that fits into any neat Marxist category; but then what revolution does? Certainly not the Russian revolution – which also had its peculiar institution (though it is an institution with many differences from the SS), that formidable organisation now known as the KGB.

One of the differences arises from the manner of the two revolutions. Some writers have denied that Nazism was revolutionary, or that Hitler made a revolution. They see him as a conservative: a radical conservative indeed, but still essentially a conservative, the agent of the German bourgeoisie. I believe that this is a shallow judgment. Admittedly, conservatives helped him to power (as did many radicals). But they soon discovered this error. He was far sharper than they. He had learned his lesson in 1923, from the fiasco of the Munich Putsch. After that mistake, he realised that the surest way to make a revolution is to come quietly and legally into power and only then to proceed to action. As Dr. Goebbels would afterwards say, before 1932 the Nazis had concealed their revolutionary aims: 'we managed to keep our political opponents from guessing our ultimate intentions and from realising that our apparent loyalty to legalistic conceptions was simply a smokescreen'. And he added – for he was speaking in 1940, the year of victory in the West – that this process would now be transferred to conquered Europe. Both stages of the process – the new order in Germany and the new order in Europe – were made possible by the SS.

The history of the SS is the history of Hitler's instrument of revolution: of the methods which he used to deceive his allies and to bring, out of an apparently conservative and legal accession to power, a radical, illegal tyranny. Throughout his reign, that tyranny grew firmer and more formidable. Had he not been defeated in war, and his entire system smashed, we would all have become subject to it: it would have made his rule permanent.

Its beginnings were small, barely perceptible. When Hitler came to power in January 1933, the SS was a mere bodyguard, subordinate to the far larger SA: that is, to the 'Brownshirts', the 'storm-troopers', who for the past twelve years had been the disorderly, violent and noisy private army of the movement. It was thanks to this 'brown army', as well as to his own oratory and promises, that Hitler had imposed himself on German politics and obliged the conservative politicians, first, to take him seriously, and then to admit him to power. But even then, they did not intend to surrender to him. They reckoned that they could control and use him for their own purposes. They saw him as their agent, the demagogue who would rally the masses to their side and so enable them to restore the unity and dignity of Germany, shattered in 1918. And indeed, but for certain events, unpredictable – or at least unpredicted – at the time, they might well have done so. If Hitler had perished before 1939, they would probably have been his heirs; and then, with skill, they might have conjured down the radical spirit which he had raised up, dismantled the machinery which he had created, and brought Germany back to an even course.

Hitler himself was well aware of this. At any moment, he declared, 'some idiot with a bomb' might succeed in assassinating him, and then what would happen to his vast programme? Only he, he insisted, had the dynamism, the vision, the charisma, and above all the iron will, to carry it through. Indeed, only he knew exactly what it was. As for his conservative allies – the generals, the old imperial officials, the bourgeoisie – he regarded them with utter contempt. They saw no further than a restoration of the Germany of 1913: its frontiers, its social structure, even its political structure. To Hitler, such ambitions were despicable in their limitation. 'Good God!' he had written in *Mein Kampf*, 'it would not be worth while to shed the blood of our people for that!'

If the conservative politicians were to control Hitler, it was essential that they sever him from his power base: that is, from his private army, the SA. Conversely, if Hitler were to preserve his independence and carry through his revolution, it was essential that he preserve such a power base. Immediately after taking office as Chancellor, he found himself faced by this problem. It was a problem which he resolved in his own way on 30 June 1934, 'the Night of the Long Knives'. On that night he bought the support of the German conservatives by destroying the SA. But he did not pay them the full price. He did not destroy his independent power-base. On the same night, by that same act of violence, he raised up a far more formidable engine of terror, the SS.

The purge of 30 June 1934 marked the break-through of the SS, the beginning of its monopoly. Originally, like the SA, it had been created as a bodyguard, to protect the infant Nazi Party against physical violence, and it had drawn its recruits, and its essential spirit, from the same source: that is, from the remains of the illegal Freikorps which had sprung up after the defeat of 1918. These Freikorps, the guerilla fighters of defeated Imperial Germany, were important as the fore-runners of Nazism, the source of its ineradicable contempt for legality.

For after 1918 there had been many Germans who refused to admit the defeat of their country as final. Most of these accepted the Weimar Republic as a necessary, if perhaps only a temporary, institution, to preserve law and order. This was the attitude, for instance, of Hindenburg, who served the Republic while hoping to change it. But the Freikorps, in their hatred of the 'November Revolution', repudiated not only the Republic but also the law and order of which it was the guarantee. They were essentially illegal; and when they had been disbanded, their illegal spirit was inherited by the SA and the SS. However, the two bodies inherited it with a difference. The SA, like the Freikorps themselves, always remained somewhat anarchical. It was also somewhat independent. Its founder, Ernst Roehm, had been an officer in the war and could afford to patronise Hitler, the corporal, whose ascendancy over his rivals, in the early days, was not yet established. The SS, founded two years later, in 1923, was Hitler's own creation, his own bodyguard; and he imposed upon it an internal discipline and a personal loyalty which made it the ideal instrument of his rising power.

Originally small in size – it was forbidden to exceed 10 per cent of the SA – the SS consisted only of local detachments available to protect Hitler or his friends on their travels in Germany. But what it lost in strength it made up in devotion. It made a virtue of 'honour', and its 'honour' – as its chosen motto declared – was unquestioning loyalty to the Führer. As Hitler gradually asserted his personal ascendancy over his early allies and rivals, so the SS, as his personal guard, grew in strength; and the SS, in turn, carried him forward towards that personal ascendancy. An important stage in this process was the appointment, in January 1929, of a new leader or Reichsführer of the SS: Heinrich Himmler.

The history of the SS, and its character, are inseparable from those of Himmler. He made it what it was to become, the engine of Hitler's power and policy. It was a double engine: an engine first of terror, then of fanaticism, of ideology. It was the instrument of repression and murder, controlling the secret police, the concentration camps, the execution squads, the gas chambers. It was also the crusading order of Nazism, preaching the doctrines of Blood and Soil, Nordic fantasy, and the conquering mission of the master race. In both capacities it was perfectly represented by Himmler, whom the world would see as the inhuman butcher of Europe but whom Hitler would describe as 'our Ignatius Loyola'.

He was a bizarre character. This pale, dim, bespectacled chicken-farmer, with his receding hair and receding chin, so scrupulous, so parsimonious, so hesitant, so mild-mannered and prim, who was so assiduous in good works, so kind to animals, so ceremonious and deferential to established rank, was at the same time the Robespierre, the sea-green incorruptible of Nazism, the methodical exterminator of whole nations. All the absurd pseudo-scientific ideas of Nazism, all the half-baked mythology of antique Teutonic heroism, all the greedy fantasies of Nordic imperialism, had been absorbed by him; and having absorbed them, he would rationalise and apply them, with text-book pedantry, on a vast scale, undismayed by the thought (for he preferred to avoid the sight) of their real meaning: millions of human beings arrested, imprisoned, tortured, starved, destroyed like vermin. And indeed, he would reply, if anyone dared to question his work, why should they not be destroyed? For were they not in fact vermin: sub-humans to be purged away from the good Germanic race which they were infecting with the virus of their inferior blood? Himmler did not pretend to like his chosen function. To exterminate vermin is not a nice job. But dirty jobs have to be done, and in the holy cause of racialism he was prepared to undertake it, and to build up an army which, being indoctrinated with his ideals, and conscious of high purpose and historical necessity, would not flinch from carrying it through: for it was an élite.

From the beginning Himmler saw his SS as an élite. Unlike the disorderly frothblowing louts of the SA, it was to be a brigade of guards, highly disciplined, closely organised, a perfect instrument adapted rationally, not brutally, to its task. It was to be a social élite too, within the party. Its uniforms were to be more elegant, its manners more correct, its discipline more hierarchical than those of the SA. It was to be an organisation which would attract scions of noble, even princely houses. And if this élite was to undertake distasteful tasks, and to carry them out with brutal efficiency, that too was a sign of its high ideal of duty: *noblesse oblige*. This perverted élitism of the SS, as created by Himmler, was noticed by many observers. As one of them stated in 1941, the SS had an ambiguous psychology: in the breast of its members 'two souls live, in strange confusion: one barbarian soul, the soul of the Nazi party, the other, a perverted aristocratic soul'.[1]

Brutality and perverted idealism: that was the essential character of the SS. The latter was represented by Himmler himself, who carried nordic mysticism to such absurd lengths. The brutality – a rationalised, economically organised, technically perfected brutality – was represented by his most formidable supporter, the intellectual technocrat of the SS, Reinhard Heydrich.

Heydrich joined the SS in 1931, two years after Himmler had become Reichsführer. He was of middle-class origin and had been a naval officer, but in 1931 he had been cashiered for impropriety: a slight which he would never forget. Ice-cold, completely amoral, without convictions or ideology, but animated by deep social and personal resentments, he found, in the SS, a new purpose for his boundless ambition. He directed his unencumbered, lucid intellect to the organisation, first, of an intelligence system for the SS, then of a rational technology of repression. Not loyalty – he was 'incapable of loyalty' – but greed for power, delight in his own clarity of mind and absolute freedom from scruples, qualified him for success in his new career. Within the SS he was hated: when he was murdered, as 'Protector of Bohemia' in 1942, a colleague in the SS would rejoice that 'that sow has gone to the butcher'; but he did more than any man under Himmler to make the SS what, to most people, it was: an engine of unqualified, unflinching, rationalised terror.

From 1931 onwards, Himmler and Heydrich built up the SS and gave it its peculiar character. But still the SS was overshadowed by the SA. If the SS protected Hitler's personal supremacy, it was the SA which terrorised the streets in the interest of the Nazi party, and ensured its electoral success. By that time the SA was once again under the command of its original founder, Ernst Roehm. Roehm had previously quarrelled with Hitler and gone as a military instructor to Bolivia, but now he had been summoned back by Hitler and had resumed his old position, chastened, as Hitler supposed, by his period of exile. But in fact it was impossible to chasten Roehm. In 1933, after Hitler had come to power, the old anarchical spirit reasserted itself. Roehm and the other SA leaders believed that it was they who had brought Hitler to power and they now expected recognition and reward. In particular, they expected that the SA, now $4\frac{1}{2}$ million strong, would become the new 'democratic' army of the Reich, displacing, as it already over-shadowed, the Reichswehr or '100,000 army' – the professional army allowed by the Treaty of Versailles.

In fact none of these things happened. Hitler, once in power, was looking forward to the next stage of his programme. He was preparing for a war of Eastern conquest. For so formidable an undertaking he needed not a mob of beer-swilling enthusiasts commanded by ill-disciplined Freikorps adventurers but an expanded professional army controlled by the old German General Staff. When Roehm and his friends found themselves and the SA neglected, they began to murmur. They spoke loosely of mutiny, of putting pressure on Hitler, of forcing him to realise where his power-base lay. They would teach him who were the real masters of the Nazi party. . . . Such was the background to the so-called 'Roehm Putsch' of 30 June 1934, which was in fact not a Putsch, or an attempted Putsch by Roehm – for the resentment of the SA never went beyond mere talk – but an anti-Roehm Putsch by Hitler, using, against the SA, his own personal instrument, which Himmler and Heydrich had rendered formidable, the SS.

[1].   Ulrich v. Hassell, *Vom andern Deutschland* (Zurich 1946) p. 240.

The 'Roehm Putsch' was one of the decisive events of Hitler's reign in Germany. It was carried out with the blessing of the Reichswehr, and, in general, of the old German establishment, who were delighted to see the destruction of the rival Brownshirt army. Many a conservative German officer who would afterwards perish in the great holocaust of 1944 openly rejoiced in that earlier holocaust of 1934. Those conservatives believed that, however violently, Hitler had destroyed the basis of his own demagogic power; that he had disarmed himself and left himself a mere politician; and that, as such, he would be absorbed and tamed by the existing political structure. They were quite wrong. The results were quite different – as time was very soon to show.

In fact, the results of the Roehm Putsch were twofold. First, with the slaughter of the SA leaders, the SS rose to be a far more formidable force than the SA had ever been. Secondly, the episode itself marked a decisive stage, psychological as well as political, in the replacement of the legal German state – that is, the responsible bureaucracy which the Weimar Republic had inherited from imperial times – by the lawless 'Führer state', the irresponsible absolute dictatorship of Hitler.

This rise of the SS and this transformation of political structure had already begun before 30 June 1934. It can be seen in Himmler's growing power over the police throughout Germany and in the establishment of the new Nazi concentration camps. The great impetus had come after the Reichstag Fire on 27 February 1933. Immediately after that fire, the communist party of Germany had been banned, and real or supposed communists had been arrested throughout the country. They were identified and arrested by the political police and thrown into the newly created camps. In the course of this process Himmler extended his control over both organisations.

Until that time, the German police had been decentralised. Each of the Länder, or constituent states, had its own police, and the political police, such as it was, was a department of the ordinary police. But ten days after the fire, Himmler was placed at the head of the Munich police, with Heydrich in charge of its political branch, was explicitly instructed not merely to maintain public order but also to secure 'loyal adherence' to Nazi rule. From that moment, a double process began: a process of centralisation and separation. First came the centralisation. In state after state the political police was placed under the control of Himmler and effectively centralised in his hands. Only Prussia eluded him – for a time; for Prussia was the personal fief of Goering, as Minister-President, who had built up in it his own 'Gestapo', or secret state police. By the summer of 1934 Himmler controlled the political police of every state except Prussia; and even in Prussia he had effective power as Deputy Chief and Inspector of the Gestapo, with Heydrich in charge of his office. Meanwhile, in state after state, the political police was severed from the ordinary police and its legal rules. It became subject to the arbitrary rule of the political party represented by Himmler.

Thanks to his control of the police, Himmler was able, at the same time, to build up the concentration camps. The original justification of the camps had been to provide 'protective custody' to political suspects – i.e. to protect them against the violence of the Nazi supporters after the Reichstag Fire. Some of these camps were official, under the Minister of the Interior; others were 'wild', i.e. unauthorised, controlled by the SA and SS. The officials of the legal state sought to enforce the law and insist on its limits to imprisonment; and indeed, by the spring of 1934, they seemed to have succeeded. New rules were formulated and many of the camps were dismantled. But then came the events of 30 June 1934, the triumph of barbarism and the SS. After that fearful purge, Himmler took over the camps formerly controlled by the SA, and neither Hitler nor he was prepared to let them go. They would never be dissolved. They would remain a permanent feature of the new, irresistible, illegal 'Führer state'.

For with that purge an irreversible step towards illegality had been taken. Hitler, as Chancellor of the Reich, and therefore political head of the legal state, had chosen to ignore law and constitution alike and to act as a mere murderer. As head of government, he had at his disposal all the administrative and coercive organs of the legal state. He had the police and the law courts. But he preferred to by-pass the legal state. Acting not as Chancellor, within the law, but as charismatic Führer, outside and above the law, he launched a *razzia* against his own people, and claimed that, as Führer, he was unaccountable to any tribunal. This was bad enough. What was worse was that he was allowed to get away with it. The German conservatives, glad to be rid of the Brownshirt army, did not lift a finger in defence of the legal state – even though some of their own friends had been included in the wholesale slaughter.

The lesson was not lost on Hitler. He saw that the legal state could be safely despised. Its natural defenders had deserted it. Thereby they had lost the moral right to appeal to it when the Führer state should turn on them, as it soon would. Meanwhile, having once begun, Hitler dismantled the legal state at will. Five weeks after the purge, President von Hindenburg died, and Hitler quietly took over his office. But he did not use his presidential powers, which were known to and regulated by the law. He would sign his decrees not as President but as 'Führer and Chancellor'. Soon he would drop the words 'and Chancellor'; for that office too was legally bounded. By ruling as Führer, a function unknown to the law, he could rule absolutely. The Reich Cabinet no longer met. The Reich Ministers no longer decided. The legal state simply withered away.

Meanwhile the SS, the organ of the illegal Führer state, was built up. In recognition of its great services, 'particularly in connection with the events of 30 June 1934', it was freed from its old subordination to the SA and declared an independent organisation. The SA, broken by the purge, sank into insignificance beside it. Having thus acquired a monopoly of power, Himmler was then able to round off his empire. By 1936 he had obtained full control of the political police in Prussia. He was then declared Reichsführer SS und Chef der Polizei. With that appointment, vainly resisted by the Minister of the Interior, the entire German police force was removed from the control of the state and incorporated into the SS. At the same time 'the orders and affairs of the Secret State Police' were declared immune from investigation by the law courts, and the concentration camps became places of execution without trial or appeal. The Minister of Justice, Franz Gürtner, once ventured to remonstrate but was quickly snubbed. The Führer, he was told, could order executions at will, by 'prerogative': it was no business of the law.[1] Gürtner's successor, Otto Thierack, drew the right conclusions: he put his office at the disposal of the SS. He invited Heydrich to 'correct' sentences by the ordinary courts and explicitly asked Himmler to take over his criminal jurisdiction over Poles, Russians, Jews and gypsies, since 'the

---

[1]. Helmut Krausnick and others, *Anatomy of the SS State*, (1968), p. 468

administration of justice can make only a small contribution to the extermination of these people'.[1]

The abdication of the legal state in favour of the Führer state – 'the SS-state' as it has been called – is the most perplexing and frightening fact in the history of Nazism. It began, I have suggested, on 30 June 1934. After that terrible failure of nerve, the process could not be reversed. The organs of the legal state survived, but only for the convenience of the Führer State: to give bureaucratic authority to its outrageous orders. So the Foreign Office facilitated the extermination of the Jews in satellite states, content if the operation was carried out in secret and described in anodyne language. The General Staff of the Armed Forces transmitted, as legitimate military orders, whatever atrocity the Führer demanded. If the generals boggled, it made no difference. They too were told to surrender their jurisdiction to those who were willing to exterminate 'these people': i.e. to the SS.

The war of 1939–45, the ultimate aim of Hitler's career, is unthinkable without the internal revolution of Germany and the absolute power exercised through the SS. The SS organised the outbreak of the war: it was Heydrich's intelligence service which fabricated the pretended Polish attack on the German radio-transmitter at Gleiwitz and it was Himmler's concentration camps which supplied the 'canned goods' – that is corpses of political prisoners, murdered for the occasion, and dressed in Polish uniforms – which were left as 'evidence' of aggression. After the invasion of Poland, it was Heydrich's SS Einsatzkommandos which followed the German armies in order to exterminate, systematically, the Polish aristocracy, intelligentsia, Jews 'and similar trash', and thereby ensure that Polish leadership should never revive. When Hitler ordered the invasion of the Soviet Union, he reckoned that the Wehrmacht might be squeamish. He therefore ordered it to stand aside and leave a free hand to the SS, which would perform its 'special tasks' of 'liquidating' all political commissars in areas otherwise under military control. And of course it was the SS which was to carry out, through 'mobile killing squads', gas-vans and extermination camps, 'the Final Solution', the destruction of the European Jews.

The horrible barbarities of Hitler's war were all the work of the SS. They constituted the special SS war, fought behind the front of the conventional war, just as the SS state rose behind the front of the legal state. But we must recognise that this SS war was not merely barbarous: it was also idealist. The barbarities were not sadistic but systematic. They were essential to Hitler's ideology, to the New Order in Europe which he was determined to set up, and which the SS, as his chosen instrument, was to realise. Few documents are so horrible as the speeches in which Himmler regularly assured the SS that, in carrying out the Final Solution, they were showing themselves a holy people, chosen above all others for their peculiar virtue to perform a sacred task, and that it was in this spirit that they must perform that task and then return, pleased with the day's work, to continue their exemplary life in other fields. The mass-murders of the SS, he insisted, were not an unfortunate by-product of war; they were not a mere pogrom (the SS disapproved of pogroms, like the so-called 'Reichskristallnacht' of 9 November 1938, organised by Goebbels and explicitly denounced by Himmler[2]); they were a historical mission, which positively sanctified those who were worthy to perform it, a mystery not to be revealed to the uncomprehending profane. The SS, said Himmler, would never talk about such things in public, but they would never hesitate to do them, if they

1. Raul Hilberg, *The Destruction of the European Jews* (Chicago, 1961) p. 644; Krausnick, op. cit. p. 81.

2. Hilberg, op. cit., p. 23.

should be necessary, and if he should order them, 'just as we never hesitated to put our erring comrades to the wall on 30 June 1934 . . .'

By the summer of 1944 the Final Solution was almost complete. Of the extermination camps, only Auschwitz would continue to operate for a few months. The rest had been dismantled, their good work done, and the signs of it were being obliterated as the Red Army advanced into Poland. But meanwhile there were other tasks for the SS, other 'erring comrades' to be put to the wall in Germany. On 20 July 1944 the German Opposition failed to assassinate Hitler. The leaders of the plot were members of the German General Staff, many of whom had connived at Hitler's own Putsch against the SA ten years earlier. Now they paid heavily for that moral and tactical error. In the terrible revenge launched against them by the SS they could reflect on the warning uttered ten years earlier to the Commander in Chief of the Army, General von Fritsch, by Captain (retired) Erwin Planck: 'if you look on without lifting a finger, you will meet the same fate sooner or later.'[1] General von Fritsch himself had met it sooner: he had been framed and destroyed by Himmler in 1938; now it was the turn of his colleagues. If the purge of the SA in 1934 had been the first of Hitler's mass-murders, the purge of the Army leaders in 1944 was the last; and both were carried out by the SS.

In 1945 Germany was at last defeated: totally defeated. With the Nazi state, the illegal, amoral, tyrannical 'Führer state', there disappeared, inevitably, the essential organ of its tyranny which was also the carrier of its justifying ideas. Perhaps nothing but total defeat could, by then, have destroyed it. But the memory of it cannot be destroyed. Not only has it perpetrated unforgettable crimes: it has also posed insoluble questions. Did it grow up naturally, out of the pressures of revolution, or was it a planned instrument of a prepared tyranny? Were its terrible achievements implicit in its formation, or did they grow out of the mere development of its power? When we look at the character of Himmler, so conventional, so mystical, so indecisive, or at the structure of Nazi government, that apparent chaos of personal satrapies, we are tempted to give one answer. When we look at the extraordinary consistency and rationality of policy, we may well give another. Large questions lie behind these answers, questions of sociology and philosophy, important to any student of politics, especially in our time; for the problem of tyranny, and the degrees and dynamics of tyranny, did not die with Hitler. There is also the question of the complicity of the German people. How far was the SS-state really distinct from the legal state? Our definitions distinguish them, but is not that an artificial distinction? Does not the one, seen as a human institution, a body of men, merge into the other? The complicity of the Reichswehr in the purge of 30 June 1934, the silence of the German conservatives, the abdication of the German political parties, the collusion of the German bureaucracy and Wehrmacht in the brutalities of the SS in the East – all these force us to ask how far the SS was entirely detachable from the German people, whether, in fact, it has not been justly described as 'the alibi of a nation'. Fortunately, we can also say that it was the alibi of a generation: a generation formed by circumstances which, we must hope, will not be repeated in the West.

Hugh Trevor-Roper, Oxford April 1976

---

[1]. Heinz Höhne, *The Order of the Death's Head* (1969) p. 128

1900-1923

HEINRICH HIMMLER

Although Himmler and the SS have become irrevocably linked, the SS began without him. Himmler was born on 7 October 1900 in Munich, into a family of solid middle-class respectability. He was named Heinrich after his godfather Prince Heinrich of Bavaria, to whom his father was tutor. Heinrich was a sickly child, who had the added misfortune of having to attend a school at which his staunchly monarchist and conservative father was headmaster

1 This photo probably taken in Füssen in 1906, shows Heinrich standing in front of his mother, Anna Maria, his older brother Gebhard on his father's left, and his youngest brother Ernst in the centre. By now Heinrich had already begun to show the meticulousness and prudishness which were to become such dominant traits in his adult character

2 On the eve of World War I the Himmlers stayed at Tittmoning, east of Munich, and here Gebhard, Heinrich (right) and Ernst were photographed with Agnes and Julie Lindner

3 Typically, Heinrich welcomed the outbreak of war with enthusiasm. During the summer of 1917, Gebhard, already serving in the Bavarian army, visited the family at Landshut, but it was not until January 1918 that Heinrich eventually reported for duty as an officer cadet in the 11th Bavarian Infantry Regiment.
4 On the 17 December 1918 he was discharged and returned to school in Landshut, where in the summer of 1919 he was photographed (second from left) with his father (fifth from left)

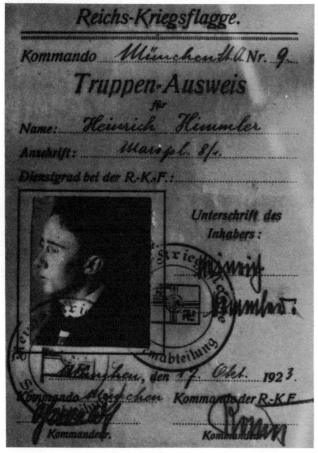

5

6

7

While preparing for a degree in agriculture at Munich Technical High School, Himmler became embroiled in right wing politics, joining first the Freikorps Oberland (5), and then the Reichskriegsflagge (6). In August 1923 he joined the National Socialist German Workers Party (NSDAP), which had been increasing in size and influence since 1920. On the eve of the Munich Putsch, in which the Nazis attempted to gain control in Bavaria, the Reichskriegsflagge was having a 'social' in the Augustiner Beer Cellar when its commander, Ernst Röhm, (19) was ordered to seize the former Reichswehr Ministry in the Leopold-strasse. The column that marched through the streets of Munich was led by Heinrich Himmler, carrying not a swastika flag, but the Imperial war flag (7). The Putsch ended in a fiasco, its leaders were arrested, and the rank and file surrendered their weapons, identified themselves to the police and went home.

The forerunner or 'mother' of the SS first appeared in Munich in March 1923, and was known as the Staff Guard (Stabswache). It was

recruited from former members of Ehrhardt's Naval Brigade, who had sworn to defend Hitler from all internal and external enemies. But Ehrhardt soon quarrelled with Hitler and withdrew his men. In May Hitler formed a new bodyguard which he called the Adolf Hitler Shock Troop

5 Himmler's identity card as a member of the Reserve Company of the Freikorps Oberland dated 25 June 1919. The Oberland Free Corps was just one of many ultra-nationalist para-military groups of demobbed soldiers, and had helped overthrow the short-lived Communist government in Munich

6 Himmler's identity card as a member of the Reichskriegsflagge, whose commander Ernst Röhm had thrown in his lot with Hitler

7 Heinrich Himmler carrying the colours of Röhm's Reichskriegsflagge, outside the Bavarian Reichswehr Ministry in the Leopoldstrasse, Munich, 9 November 1923

8 The Adolf Hitler Shock Troop leaving for the German Day in Bayreuth, 2 September 1923. Leaning on the cab is its first commander Joseph Berchtold; behind the flag Ulrich Graf, and with goggles, Julius Schreck

1924-1932

Following the Putsch, the NSDAP was banned and Hitler imprisoned. On his release on 20 December 1924 he began to re-build his party, and in February 1925 the NSDAP was reconstituted. In April Hitler formed a new eight-man bodyguard or Stabswache, which officially became the Schutzstaffel (Protection Squad) or SS on 9 November 1925

9 The Führer heads a propaganda march through the streets of Weimar in July 1926. L to R (left to right): Strasser, Schwarz, Hitler, Rosenberg, Generalleutnant a.D.Heinemann, Hess and Heinrich Himmler

10 Julius Schreck (in centre with moustache) and his Stabswache, summer 1925

11 Hitler and four of his first SS men (a fifth has been erased). L to R: Schaub, Schreck, Hitler, Maurer, and Schneider. The fifth man was Emil Maurice who was thrown out of the SS in 1935 when found to be a Jew, but later allowed to retain his appointments and privileges, and wear SS uniform

10

12 In June 1924 Himmler began to work as secretary to the Regional Leader (Gauleiter) of the lower Bavarian branch of the National Socialist Freedom Movement, Gregor Strasser. By tireless and efficient handling of all routine matters Himmler soon made himself indispensable, and lower Bavaria one of the best organised regions. In this photo Otto Strasser (bareheaded in brown shirt), Chief of Staff of the SA Pfeffer von Salomon (in brown cap), and Himmler pose with the Landshut SS, summer 1926
13 Goebbels addresses a political meeting in Berlin in 1926, while SS men stand guard. The main role of the SS at this period was the protection of meetings in its area, recruitment of

subscribers and advertisers for the party newspaper *Völkischer Beobachter*, and the recruitment of party members

In February 1925 Strasser agreed to disband his party and join the reconstituted NSDAP. Himmler now found himself a local Nazi Party official with command over the tiny SS in his district. In September 1926 Strasser was appointed Reich Propaganda Leader of the NSDAP, and Himmler followed him to party headquarters as his secretary. Himmlers' organising abilities did not go unnoticed and in 1927 he was appointed Deputy Leader, and in January 1929 National SS Leader (Reichsführer-SS), which by then

13

12

14 Hitler takes refreshment in a beer garden while his SS bodyguard insulate him from onlookers. Round the table clockwise are Hitler's photographer Heinrich Hoffmann, Berchtold, unidentified, and Hitler, summer 1925

14

had risen to one thousand men. To the SA this colourless bureaucrat posed little threat; he was just the man to command the SS and assure its continued subordination to the SA In September 1925 Julius Schreck sent a circular letter to all regional groups of the NSDAP asking them to form an SS, the strength of which was fixed by the SA at one officer and ten men. This was the beginning of the so-called 'Zehnerstaffel' or Groups of Ten. Not anybody could join, because the seeds of élitism had already been sown. Applicants had to be between twenty-five and thirty-five, have two sponsors, be registered with the police as residents of five years standing, and be strong and healthy. Habitual

drunkards, gossip-mongers and other delinquents were not to be admitted. The reason was simple: Hitler and his followers were tirelessly campaigning to increase membership of the NSDAP and were beginning to travel outside Bavaria, into areas where allegiance was local, rather than to Hitler himself. Hitler needed a small handpicked bodyguard on which he could rely completely wherever he went. To distinguish the SS from the SA, SS men began to wear black caps and ties, and black edging to their swastika armbands The SS was still nominally under SA command, but its leader Julius Schreck (15) was considered too easy-going, and did not carry the weight to ensure

that the SS remained the movement's élite force. So Schreck was replaced by Berchtold who was appointed National Leader of the SS (Reichs-führer-SS). In March 1927 he too resigned in favour of his deputy Eduard Heiden. The SA kept a jealous eye on SS expansion, and local SA commanders often used the SS for the most demeaning tasks, nor was the SS allowed to form units in towns where the SA was under strength, nor recruit more than ten per cent of the strength of the SA. By 1928 the SS had still only 280 members

15

16

15 Hitler and his 'Chauffeureska'.
L to R: Ulrich Graf (who saved Hitler's life on 9 November 1923), Rudolf Hess, Julius Schaub, Adolf Hitler, and Dr Friedrich Weber, 1929
16 Hitler speaks for the first time in the Berlin concert house Clou to a crowd of 5,000. When this photo was taken a uniform ban was in force, and Hitler's chauffeur and bodyguard Julius Schreck (in peaked cap) wears plain clothes, 1 May 1927
17 Himmler's SS leaders' identity card as Reichsführer-SS, issued after 6 January 1929
18 Josef 'Sepp' Dietrich in the uniform of an SS Colonel (Standartenführer). A former tank n.c.o. in World War 1, butcher, and chucker-out, Dietrich was one of Hitler's original bodyguards, autumn 1930

17

18

19 Captain Ernst Röhm as Chief of Staff (Stabschef) of the SA, 1931

20 On 1 July 1932 all Austrian SA and SS units assembled in Linz in upper Austria for an inspection by Adolf Hitler, SA Chief Göring, General Franz Ritter von Epp, and Graf du Moulin Eckhardt. The SS man (2nd from right front row) is none other than Ernst Kaltenbrunner (344) The early 1930's was a period of extreme political violence. Nazis, Communists and Monarchists beat up each other's newspaper sellers, staged provocative marches, and fought pitched battles in which 'india rubbers' (coshes) and 'match boxes' (pistols) were frequently used. It was in this supercharged atmosphere of violence that so many men, embittered by defeat and depression, came to join the SS, and it was this emphasis on physical toughness and swagger that came to characterise the SS

20

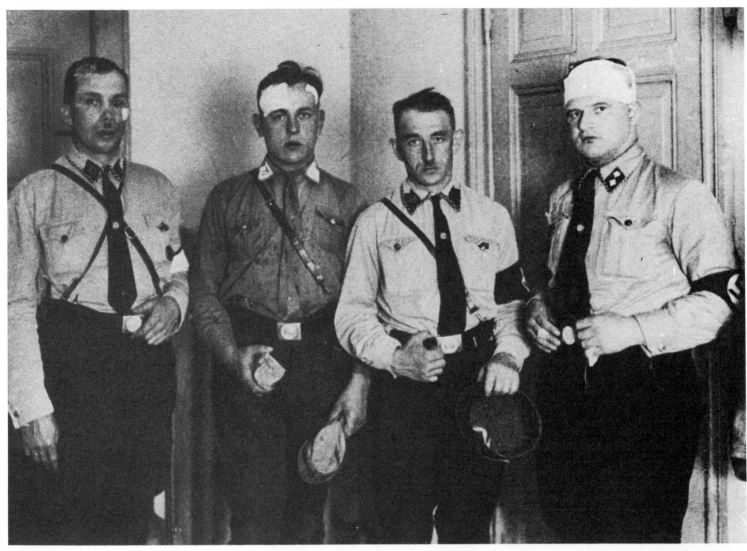

21 Wounded members of the Danzig
SA and SS photographed after the
bloody riots which became known as
'Totensonntag' (Death Sunday),
November 1931
22 Funeral of an SS man killed by
the Communists, Berlin 1932
23 The Communist equivalent of the
SA was the Red Front Fighters'
Association (Rötfrontkämpferbund)
24 Hitler congratulates an SA man
wounded in a street fight, 1932
25 When Chancellor Brüning banned
political uniforms the Pfalz SS paraded
half-naked, Germesheim, April 1932

22

23

24

25

26 Reichstag President Göring and Himmler on the way to the Reichstag. Although looking relaxed enough it was known that Göring cordially loathed the prim and servile 'Reichs Heini'

27 Gauleiter of Berlin Dr Joseph Goebbels addresses a meeting in the Berlin Sports Palace as part of the electoral campaign. Many Berlin SA men were excluded from the list of Nazi candidates, because they were either too ignorant or too radical or both, and so the SA refused to help keep order and left in the middle of the meeting

27

1933

28 As the crucial 1933 general elections approached it suited the Nazis to create the impression that Germany was on the verge of anarchy. On 22 January 1933 the Berlin SA staged a provocative march past the Communist Party headquarters in Bülowplatz. Police with armoured cars were called out in force but this time the Communists ignored the challenge

29 In February 1933 Göring called out 15,000 Berlin SA and SS men to act as auxiliary police, and in so doing released a wave of terror. Communists and Social Democrats were herded into makeshift prisons where they were beaten and tortured. By the end of the month some 4,000 political prisoners were under lock and key

30

31

30 Hitler was one of the first politicians to make extensive use of air travel during an election campaign. On arrival at Königsberg in East Prussia he was accompanied by his bodyguard Dietrich, and commander of the local SS regiment Ihle. Bringing up the rear is the honorary SA-Oberführer Prince August Wilhelm of Prussia

31 On 21 March 1933 the new National Socialist Reichstag opened in the Kroll Opera House (the Reichstag building having been burnt down). Over their swastika armbands the SS men wear a mourning band

32 Hitler addresses the Reichstag for the first time as Chancellor. Prussian Minister of the Interior Wilhelm Frick, like many of the other Nazi delegates, looked forward to 'a strong government, unhampered by individuals, groups, classes, privileges, parties, or parliaments', and they were not to be disappointed

33 A joyous crowd in the Wilhelm-strasse besieges Hitler's car, January 1933 Hitler did not reward Himmler with a ministerial post, but 1933 marked the turning point in his career. On 1 April he became Commander of the Bavarian Political Police, and now that he had the necessary executive powers he began to wage a relentless war on the opposition

34 Himmler with his superior General Franz Ritter von Epp, State Governor of Bavaria. Epp was a deeply religious man and was later to criticise the SS for 'undermining the confidence in the law, which is the foundation of every state'. March 1933

35 Himmler's Bavarian hunting permit as Police President of Munich, April 1933

36 Police officials and SS auxiliary policemen, check the papers of Jews taken into protective custody during the pogroms of March 1933

37 Jewish-owned businesses were daubed, and SA and SS men prevented customers from entering, Berlin 1933

38 A group of SS men prepare to burn Communist banners and placards.

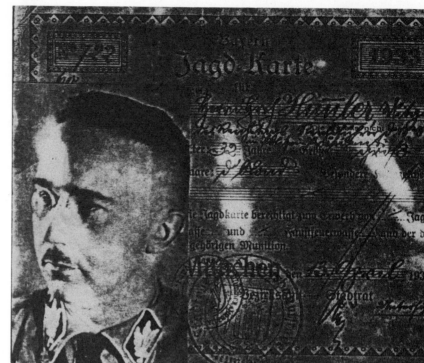

35

34   36

HEITINGER

Jude! Jude Jude Jude! Jude!

37

ROT-FREIHEIT

Schützt
SowJet
Russland

38

Konzentrationslager für Schutzhäftlinge in Bayern

39

THE WILD CAMPS

The Ordinance for the Protection of People and State, which was passed on 28 February 1933 – the day after the Reichstag fire – empowered the Police Presidents to take into protective custody anyone considered to be a political opponent in the widest sense of the term. Makeshift camps sprung up all over Germany. Lack of supervision and the frightful stories of brutality which leaked from them led them to be called 'wild' camps. By the end of July 1933 it was estimated that there were nearly 27,000 people being held in protective custody. By May 1934 most of the wild camps had been closed, and the remainder reorganised and unified under SS control

39 The headline of the 21 March 1933 issue of the *Völkischer Beobachter* announced the opening of a new camp in Bavaria with a capacity of 5,000 prisoners. At first Dachau was much the same as any other camp, where in order to have a roof over their head the inmates had to build it themselves
40 In June 1934 the former Army paymaster and psychiatric clinic patient, Theodor Eicke, became

40

41   42

43

commander of Dachau, and set about turning it into a 'model' camp. He formulated the code for guards and inmates which was to become standard throughout the concentration camp system. This photo shows the Dachau guard detachment which was 'drawn from the stupidest and most indolent section of the population who, when unemployment ended, saw no way of avoiding doing a decent job of work other than by joining the SS'. Within weeks Eicke had fired sixty of them, and began to hand-pick his men

41 Until productive employment could be organised inmates flattened the stony parade ground and internal roads with a heavy water-filled roller, which provided many hours of back-breaking toil, May 1933

42 While their SA guards look on, inmates peel potatoes in Oranienburg camp near Berlin. The camp routine was based on that of the German Army with reveille at 05.30, and lights out at 17.00 hours

43 The entrance to Sachsenburg concentration camp in Thuringia, 1933

44 Oranienburg camp money paid to inmates to enable them to purchase exorbitantly priced necessities in the camp canteen, 1933

44

BLUT UND BODEN

In June 1933 Himmler's protégé SS-Gruppenführer Darré became Reich Minister of Food and Prussian Minister of Agriculture. Darré was an Argentine German educated at King's College School in Wimbledon, England. He first met Himmler when both were members of the Artamanen — a sort of back-to-nature branch of the Völkisch German Youth Movement. Darré implanted in Himmler the 'blood and soil' and 'glorification of the peasant' theories which became cornerstones of SS philosophy. Since 1931 Darré had dealt with all SS matters relating to agriculture, race, and marriage through the newly formed SS Race and Resettlement Main Office

45 Himmler and Darré meet farmers from Miesbach in upper Bavaria. Darré firmly believed that 'peasants had always formed the only reliable basis for our people from the point of view of blood'

46 Darré with regionally costumed peasants from upper Franconia at the first Reich Farmer's Day held at Weimar, 19–21 January 1934

45

46

47 Through his personal adjutant
Karl Wolff and other well-connected
SS officers, Himmler began to
cultivate the aristocracy and
industrialists, and encouraged them to
join the SS. Here Himmler hunts with
Willy Sachs (grandfather of the
well-known playboy Gunther) and
Ritter von Epp. At this time Wolff (on
the right) was already in the SS, but
was acting as Epp's adjutant,
Oberaudorf, summer 1934

As already described the SS originated as a small band of bodyguards. By mid-1933 SS membership had increased to 11,000 of which only roughly ten per cent (on the staff) were regulars. The remainder were part-timers, who met once or twice a week (usually on Sundays) for training and indoctrination sessions, which inevitably ended in a booze-up. They went on an annual camp, and could be called out in emergencies in support of the police for route lining and crowd control, and in the event of internal disorder. In many respects the pre-war activities of the bulk of the SS can be compared to those of a Boy Scout, and the average SS man, too young to have served in World War 1, had about as much military know-how.

It soon became apparent to the Nazi hierarchy that apart from its rather unwieldy para-military formations, which in the main were unarmed, it had no force capable of protecting them from a determined coup. So from May 1933 a number of company-sized SS detachments were armed and put on a full-time footing. They were at first known as Special Commandos then Political Readiness Squads, and finally as the Waffen-SS

48 Hitler addresses a political meeting in the Sports Palace in Berlin, and for the first time is guarded not by ordinary SS men but by a full-time armed bodyguard or Stabswache, 8 April 1933
49 Here men of the Sonderkommando Zossen (better known later as the Leibstandarte-SS) undergo military training in Essenfassen, summer 1933

49

48

50 On 6 May 1933 the Nazis began an action against unwanted books. Together with the pseudo-scientific pornography so popular in Germany at the time, many important literary works were proscribed because their authors or subjects were considered subversive or un-German

51 The cover of the programme for the 1st SS *'Appell'* of Group East in Berlin

53 The leader of SS Group East was the pig-headed SS-Gruppenführer Daluege who, despite limited intelligence (nicknamed Dummi-Dummi) had with Göring's protection acquired considerable powers and was so strong that he refused to deal with anyone but Hitler and Röhm, and certainly not with that Bavarian chicken-breeder Himmler

54 At midday on 13 August the Chief of Staff of the SA Röhm and his subordinate Himmler inspected the Berlin SS. In this photo an incident has obviously just taken place — possibly a shouted insult at the notorious homosexual Röhm. L to R: Daluege, Heines, Himmler, Waldeck und Pyrmont, and Röhm.

1. Schutzstaffel-
Appell
der Gruppe Oft in Berlin
11.12.13. August

52 From 11 to 13 August 1933 SS
Group East held its first big rally in the
German stadium in Berlin. The SS
camp was at nearby Döberitz, where
Himmler's quarters consisted of a tent
and bales of straw

53

54

After Hitler's seizure of power, a rapid return to normalisation and an end to further 'revolutionary' activity was recommended if the economy of the country was to be stabilised. Following the successful July 1935 'elections' 6,000 political prisoners — mainly rank and file Communists — were pardoned and released from concentration camps

55 SS Brigadeführer Theodor Eicke, who often told his men that 'there is no place in the ranks of the SS for men with soft hearts and any such would do well to retire quickly to a monastery', inspects a batch of pardoned prisoners, Dachau, 19 November 1933

56 Under the watchful eye of the SS duty n.c.o. prisoners sign their discharge papers

57 A clerk hands out the discharge papers

58 A pardoned prisoner takes leave of his guards with a handshake. This 'spontaneous' photograph was intended to convey 'no hard feelings', which may have been the attitude of most Germans, but certainly did not apply to the SS, who often waited outside non-SS camps to re-arrest the more recalcitrant released prisoners

59 The gates of Dachau camp swing open on 12 November 1933 to let prisoners out in time for Christmas, but former membership of the Communist party and a concentration camp past were difficult to live down in Nazi Germany

57

58

59

1934 THE NIGHT OF THE LONG KNIVES

Very early on in the history of the Nazi movement, a conflict arose between those like Hitler who wished to gain power constitutionally, and those represented by the SA who wished to do away with the old established institutions, including the German Army, with those of their own making

60 Himmler and Rudolf Diels, the first chief of the Gestapo appointed by Göring in 1932. Diels was no Nazi, and throughout 1933 waged an incessant war against the illegal activities of the Berlin SA and SS. In the autumn of 1933 he realised that he was fighting a losing battle and left the country. He was later reconciled with Himmler who allowed him to wear the uniform of an honorary SS-Standartenführer (Colonel)

In 1931 Himmler appointed a cashiered Naval signals officer, Reinhard Heydrich to create an SS intelligence service. At first it was known as the Ic (intelligence) desk at Himmler's headquarters and, during the ban on the SA and SS, as the Press and Information Service. Under Heydrich's skilful and ruthless guidance it gradually established itself as the sole intelligence service of the NSDAP. In April 1934 Heydrich finally took command of the Prussian Gestapo
61 On January 1933 Himmler, Hitler, and Röhm attended a concert together in the Berlin Sports Palace
62 SS-Brigadeführer (Brigadier) Heydrich as commander of the Bavarian Political Police in his Munich office in April 1934. At this time he was gathering incriminating evidence against the SA

Long denied a position in the State to which it felt entitled the SA was bitter, but not on the verge of open revolt. The SS however convinced Hitler that it was, and with Army backing prepared quietly for a showdown. Hitler was still hesitant, but the Army told him in no uncertain terms that if he wanted its support Röhm must go and the SA be cut down to size. By 25 June Hitler had made up his mind. On 30 June began a carefully co-ordinated operation which ended two days later with the death, not only of Röhm and 16 senior SA commanders, but a further 66 victims who had for one reason or another fallen foul of the SS

65

63

64

63 SA-Obergruppenführer Krüger, director of SA training, supplied the SS with incriminating evidence. The SA detested him for his treachery, and the SS came to consider him a scandalmonger and a pedant

64 As a reward for his treachery SA-Obergruppenführer Viktor Lutze was made chief of staff of the SA, but he was never to forgive the SS for its treatment of the SA during the purge

65 The Reichswehr was delighted with the elimination of SA power, but as yet did not recognise the much more subtle threat offered by the SS. When told of the shooting of the SA leaders, General von Witzleben rubbed his hands together and said 'what a pity, I ought to have been there'. Here SS and military leaders hold a 'comradely evening' at the old Military Academy in Berlin. L to R: Dietrich, Witzleben (executed after the Bomb Plot), Fisch, Weitzel, Förster, von Bock, and Halm

On 20 July 1934 Hitler declared the SS an independent formation of the NSDAP, and removed it from SA control. Its position of ascendency was now assured, and it entered a period of consolidation in which it developed its command structure, armed units, concentration camps, and security service, while at the same time shedding some 60,000 SS men who had been recruited at a time when the SS was competing for members with the SA, but who now did not conform to the SS image

66 On his return to Berlin, Hitler appeared at the window of his new Chancellery to acknowledge the cheers of the crowd. Below him stand members of the security guard, who were responsible for his safety, July 1934

66

TRIUMPH OF THE WILL

The highlight of the National Socialist calendar was the Nuremberg Rally or 'Parteitag' which was held each year in September. The sixth rally held in 1934 was called 'Triumph of the Will' and was the largest so far. Its mixture of medieval pageant and scout jamboree made an enormous impression, not only on the German participants, but also on the spectators who included many foreigners

67 (top to bottom) aerial view of the Hitler Youth camp, SS kitchens, and mealtime for the SS contingent
68 Hitler discusses the filming of the rally with L to R: Lutze, Schaub, and Leni Riefenstahl

69

70

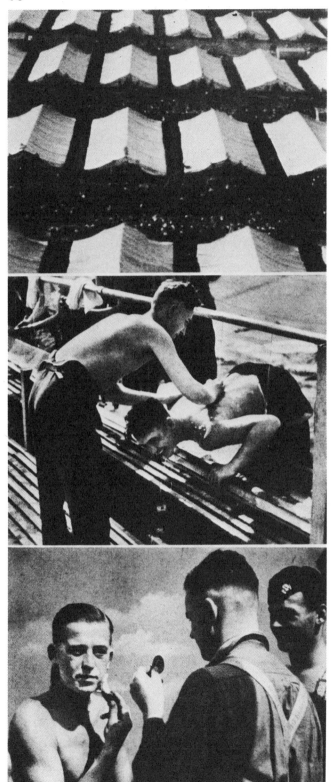

69 Hitler flanked by Himmler and
Lütze face the Memorial to the Dead
(Totenehrung), and the Blood Flag
70 Reveille in the SS camp.
Organisation on this scale was a huge
undertaking; by 1939 the orders for
the SS contingent alone ran to 160
pages

71 On 20 January 1935 the great SS leaders' conference was held in Breslau. The original British caption to this press photograph gives an interesting example of the British policy of appeasement. It suggests that 'Germany's secret police are not always the sinister beings they are supposed to be', and shows 'the happy faces of the SS chief and his men as they arrive at the meeting'

72 On 13 January 1935 the inhabitants of the Saar voted overwhelmingly to return to the Reich, and for the first time an armed SS unit marched alongside the German Army, Saarbrücken, 1 March 1935

At Himmler's instigation the SS began a 'Germanic' revival, and spent large sums on restoration of ancient monuments and on archaeological excavations. Hitler was not amused and told Speer 'Himmler is starting to dig up these villages of mud huts and enthusing over every potsherd and stone axe he finds. All we prove by that is that we were still throwing stone hatchets and crouching round open fires when Greece and Rome had already reached the highest stage of culture'

73 SS musicians blowing ancient northern German lurs at a Norse Music Festival, June 1935

71

72

1935

In 1935 the command structure of the SS was enlarged by the formation of the SS Main Office (SS-Hauptamt), with inspectorates for the armed SS and Death's Head formations. Darré's Race and Resettlement Office was given main office status. Two cadet schools were established at Bad Tölz and Braunschweig where a new generation of SS officers was to be trained in the SS spirit. In March conscription was re-introduced, as well as compulsory service in the Reich Labour Corps

74 In the summer Hitler, having driven through hundreds of harvest arches in the villages en route, visits the annual Harvest Festival at Bückeberg. On arrival he has to forge his way through a heaving and sweaty crowd to award farmers and their families with the harvest crown before an altar laden with fruits of the earth
75 This party member is overcome with heat, but in villages all over Germany Nazi village bigwigs become inebriated with their own verbosity and alcohol, Bückeberg, 7 October 1935
76 A new fox-hunting club was founded by the Ministry of the Interior, and opened its first season near Berlin on 3 September 1935. In the centre of the photograph in SS uniform is the Master of the Hunt, State Secretary SS-Brigadeführer Grauert and on his right in Naval uniform, Admiral Canaris, head of military intelligence (Abwehr)

77 Massed SS standards at the seventh Party Congress (Party Day of Freedom). It was here that the new Reich Citizen's Law, and Law for the Protection of German Blood and German Honour (known thereafter as the Nuremberg Laws) were proclaimed, 10 September 1935
78 Himmler with his adjutant Karl Wolff, and Reinhard Heydrich, on Himmler's birthday outing on the Tegernsee, 7 October 1935
79 The original Reich Chancellery guard was drawn from the Army's Berlin Guard Battalion, but it was thought wiser to replace it by a new one drawn from the Leibstandarte-SS, here seen changing guard in the courtyard of the old Chancellery, summer 1935

78

79

1936

80

81

80 The former Army officer and champagne salesman Joachim von Ribbentrop was given honorary SS rank in May 1933, when he became Hitler's special adviser on foreign affairs, and finally in 1938 Foreign Minister. Himmler considered it a major prestige victory for the SS uniform to be seen in that bastion of conservatism, the Foreign Office. Here Ribbentrop walks with his family and SS bodyguards near his Dahlem home, spring 1936

81 In December 1936 the Chief of the military intelligence service (Abwehr) Admiral Canaris, and chief of the SS Security Service Reinhard Heydrich concluded a pact which became known as the 'Ten Commandments'. Abwehr was to continue to deal with espionage abroad and counter-espionage at home, while the SD (and Gestapo) was to deal with internal enemies; but it was not to be so. Here Canaris and Heydrich dine out together in Berlin; although professionally bitter enemies, social relations were cordial since both shared a Naval background and a love of music.

82 Another SS innovation was the 'Circle of Friends of the Reichsführer-SS'. It was composed of wealthy industrialists who were expected to make regular financial contributions towards cultural, social, and charitable activities of the SS. In return they hoped to benefit from SS favour and protection. Here Dietrich takes a group of 'friends' on a tour of his barracks in Berlin-Lichterfelde. L to R: Army Medical Inspector Generalarzt Dr Waldmann, SS-Standartenführer d'Alquen, Dr Schmidt, a Hannovarian lawyer, General Director Röhnert of the Lüdenscheid Metal Works, Dietrich, SS-Obersturmführer Dr Voss, Director of the Deutschen Revisions-u. Treuhandgesellschaft, Dr Rasche Director of the Dresdener Bank, with behind honorary SS-Standarten-führer Graf Gottfried von Bismarck, Oberbürgermeister of Berlin Dr Lippert, Dr Ritter von Halt Director of the Deutsche Bank, and Secretary of State and honorary SS-Gruppenführer Keppler

83 On Hitler's birthday lorry loads of presents would arrive at the Chancellery, where additional SS men were called in to help unload, while inside security men checked the contents to see that the gifts were not booby-trapped, 20 April 1936

82

83

84 SS men undergo instruction in the Runic alphabet, summer 1936

85 On 16 May 1936 Julius Schreck, Hitler's driver and first commander of the SS, died. Hitler described him to Speer as 'the best driver you can imagine; and our supercharger is good for over a hundred. We always drove very fast. But in recent years I've told Schreck not to go over fifty. How terrible if something had happened to me'. Schreck is on the right, and Hermann Fegelein in the centre

In March the 3,500 concentration camp guards were re-organised as the Death's Head Formations (SS-Totenkopfverbände), and in April they were removed from General SS control. The scruffy and ill-disciplined guards (40) that Eicke had found in 1933, had by 1937 become almost indistinguishable, apart from the death's head on their collar patch, from the other highly disciplined units of the armed SS

86 On 8 May 1936 Himmler conducted a group of Nazi party officials around Dachau concentration camp, of which he was becoming inordinately proud

87 When routes had to be lined the uniformed formations of the NSDAP, and particularly the SS were called out. Although it made a welcome change from factory bench the amount of time spent in party activities had its effect on the economy. Here men of the 75th SS Foot Regiment (Berlin) line the route on May Day, which was now renamed 'Day of National Labour', 1 May 1936

85

86

HENRY THE FOWLER

On the thousandth anniversary of the death of King Heinrich I (875–936), Himmler participated in a solemn ceremony of his own making in the crypt of Quedlinburg Cathedral. The Saxon King Heinrich (Henry the Fowler) had defeated the Slavs, and his namesake Heinrich came to regard himself as the reincarnation of this warrior king and founder of the German Reich. In 1937 he had the bones of Heinrich I transferred to the tomb in the Cathedral which previously had lain empty

88 An engraving of Heinrich I by an unknown SS artist entitled 'Eternity of the Reich'
89 Badge struck to commemorate the thousandth anniversary
90 Himmler lays a wreath on the empty tomb of Heinrich I in the Quedlinburg Cathedral, 2 July 1936

88

Ewig das Reich

89

90

91 Oberbürgermeister Selig of
Paderborn, assisted by an aged
SA n.c.o., places a commemorative
scroll in a sandstone container at the
SS castle in Wewelsburg, near
Paderborn

91

92 Hitler arrives at Bayreuth to open the annual Wagner Festival. He tried to go each year, and claimed that Wagner's music was a great source of inspiration to him. Winifred Wagner still remembers his visits with pleasure and claims that if he turned up today she would be as pleased as ever to greet him

93 By decree of the Führer the party post of Reichsführer-SS was formally amalgamated with the newly established government post of Chief of the German Police. In this photograph Himmler shows the new uniforms for the first national German police force to Hitler. Behind Hitler is Minister of the Interior, Dr Wilhelm Frick, 20 June 1936

94 Communications are essential to the smooth running of a police state, and so the standard of radio communications in the SS was at least as good, if not better, than that of the German armed forces. Here members of the SS Signals Battalion take a rest during the 1936 Olympic Games in Berlin

93

94

MEINE EHRE HEISST TREUE

95 All graduates of the SS cadet schools were automatically presented with the SS sword, together with a citation which exhorted its recipient to 'never draw it without reason, or sheath it without honour'. Senior SS leaders received a sword of honour from Himmler personally, which bore a dedication and his signature on the blade

96 The anniversay of the 9 November 1923 Putsch was a national holiday; the most sacred day in the National Socialist Calendar. It was a day of solemn marches by survivors of the Putsch, parades, and speeches. It ended in front of the Feldherrnhalle in Munich with the swearing-in of armed SS candidates. Here they took the oath of allegiance to Hitler, and swore to observe the fundamental laws of the SS. Then the SS man was entitled to wear the SS dagger with which he was expected to defend his honour in accordance with the code of honour of the black corps

Der Reichsführer-SS   Nürnberg, 13. September 1936

SS-Untersturmführer

B ö h m e r Karl , SS-Nr.161 334.

Ich verleihe Ihnen den Degen der SS

Ziehen Sie ihn niemals ohne Not!
Stecken Sie ihn niemals ein ohne Ehre!

Wahren Sie Ihre eigene Ehre ebenso bedingungslos, wie Sie die Ehre anderer zu achten und für Schutzlose ritterlich einzutreten haben!

Dieser Degen soll in Ihrer Sippe Besitz verbleiben, wenn Sie ihn ein Leben lang untadelig getragen haben. Scheiden Sie vorher aus der SS aus, so fällt er zurück an den Reichsführer-SS.

Vergessen Sie keinen Augenblick, welch großes Vertrauen die Schutzstaffel Adolf Hitlers Ihnen durch Verleihung dieser Waffe geschenkt hat. Bleiben Sie in guten und schlechten Tagen immer der gleiche!

Führen Sie den Degen in Ehren!

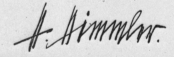

95

96

97

97 Himmler presents the SS sword to newly commissioned officers, 1937
98 The cult of the sword is evoked in this photograph of an SS officer showing his sword to a suitably overawed member of Hitler's Young Folk

98

1937

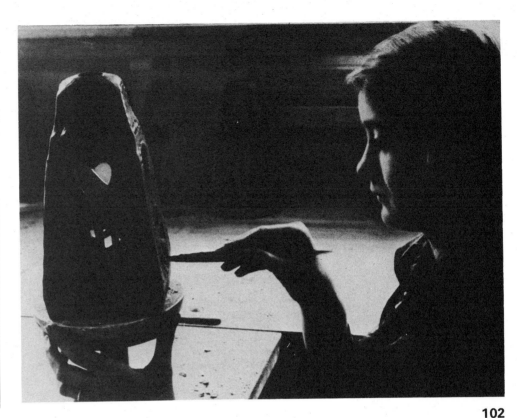

102

One of the first economic enterprises begun by the SS was the acquisition of a small porcelain factory in Allach. In 1937 it was moved to the SS complex at Dachau, where it produced high quality porcelain and official SS gifts, such as the pseudo-Germanic Yuletide candle holder (*Julleuchter*). The artistic director of the works was Carl Diebitsch, who was also responsible for the design of SS uniforms, insignia, and coats of arms for senior SS leaders

99 In 1937 the 'Friends of the Reichsführer-SS' were taken on a tour of the Gestapo Museum of Free Masonry in the Masonic Lodge in Nuremberg. L to R: (back to camera) Karl Wolff, unidentified, General Director Lindemann, Chief of the Potash Syndicate Rosterg, Secretary of State and Minister of Transport Kleinmann, and General Director Röhnert

100 In February 1937, Osnabrück played host to its old comrades serving in the SS. A day of wreath-laying and speeches ends in the obligatory *'Kameradschaftsabend'* in the local brewery

101 Here German musicians and singers attend the opening of an exhibition of SS porcelain in Berlin. Diebitsch is on the left

102 The production line at the SS porcelain factory in Dachau. Here a young girl puts the finishing touches to a Julleuchter

103 At the NSDAP Ski Championships in Rottach-Egern, the SS won the Führer's Prize, and Himmler and Reich Sport Minister von Tschammer und Osten were present to award it, February 1937

In 1937 began in earnest the process of merging the police with the SS into what was to become the 'State Protection Corps'. The SS now consisted of three distinct branches, each with its own command structure: the SS-Verfügungstruppe or armed SS, the SS-Totenkopfverbände or concentration camp guards, and Security Police which combined the SS Security Service and Gestapo. The remainder – now numbering some 240,000 men – was known as the Allgemeine or General SS. The concentration camps underwent a further re-organisation. The five battalions of guards became three regiments with a strength of 4,449 men, and the seven camps were re-organised as three main or 'Hauptlager'. In August the first camp for women was set up in Lichtenberg. The SD was cock-a-hoop with the results of its first foray into Abwehr territory, when it received confirmation that Soviet Marshall Tukhachevski had been tried and executed for treason. It is now known that Stalin had already decided to purge his officer corps, and that the forged documents implicating Tukhachevski which the SD planted were just the excuse he was looking for

104 Hitler receives the good wishes, and an expensive hand-made SS sword bearing the inscription 'In good times and bad, we will always be the same', from the leadership corps of the SS. L to R: Dietrich, Himmler, and the chiefs of the main offices Darré (race) Daluege (police) Lorenz (ethnic Germans), Heydrich (security), Schmitt (personnel) and Karl Wolff, 20 April 1937
105 During the celebrations to mark the founding of the Nazi Party in Augsburg, Hitler drove under a triumphal arch bearing the slogan 'Victory to the Führer' before again demanding colonial living room — 'we must raise the cry louder and louder, so that the world will not be able to refuse to hear it', 24 November 1937

106 Hitler's modest mountain retreat was converted over the years into a huge governmental complex enclosed with a nine-mile-long outer fence, and guarded by a detachment of Leibstandarte

107 This happy couple photographed soon after their open-air marriage under a lime tree are Karl 'Karli' Koch, commandant of Esterwegen and later Buchenwald concentration camps, and his bride Ilse. Despite Himmler's continuous preaching about SS honour and integrity, Koch and others like him grew exceedingly rich out of the concentration camp system. But Koch went too far, and was tried and executed shortly before the end of the war. His wife went on to become the infamous 'Bitch of Buchenwald' (351)

1938

108 Himmler with his wife Marga and daughter Gudrun in 1938. Marga was eight years older than Heinrich and a Protestant. After presenting her to his parents for the first time he told his brother Gebhard 'I'd rather clear a hall of a thousand Communists single-handed than go through that again'. The marriage was not a success and soon after the birth of Gudrun they began to live apart. He then formed a relationship with one of his former secretaries, Hedwig Potthast, who stayed with him to the end and bore him two more daughters

109 Heinrich Himmler with his daughter Gudrun at an indoor sports meeting in Berlin, March 1938. Today Gudrun lives in Munich and still remembers him as 'a kindly man and the best father'

110 The Leibstandarte-SS march past its Führer on the fifth annive of the assumption of power, 30 January 1938

108

109

THE BLOMBERG-FRITSCH AFFAIR

In 1938 the Army's two most senior and respected officers, Field-Marshal Werner von Blomberg and Werner Freiherr von Fritsch fell victims to Heydrich's intrigues. Fritsch, who had resisted all attempts at armed expansion within the SS, was accused of a homosexual offence. Blomberg the arch-conservative was revealed to have recently married the daughter of a brothel-keeper. Fritsch was eventually tried by courts martial and acquitted on all counts; Blomberg was forced into retirement. The Gestapo was discredited and anti-SS feeling was running so high in the Army that Heydrich was convinced that it would march on the Prinz-Albrecht-Strasse. It didn't, but, then it didn't quite realise what far-reaching repercussions the Blomberg-Fritsch affair would have: sixteen generals were retired, and another forty-four were posted. The War Ministry was transformed into the Oberkommando der Wehrmacht and Hitler appointed himself Commander-in-Chief. Nor was the other 'conservative' institution to escape a shake-up. The career diplomat and Foreign Minister, von Neurath, was replaced by the outsider and honorary SS-Gruppenführer Joachim von Ribbentrop (or 'brickendrop' as he was known in the English press). On 5 February 1938 the headlines of the *Völkischer Beobachter* announced 'strongest concentration of all power in the Führer's hands' and, as William Shirer pointed out, this time the leading Nazi daily was not exaggerating.

111 Blomberg (left) and Fritsch in the Marktplatz, Nuremberg, 13 September 1937
112 The Leibstandarte-SS 'Adolf Hitler' marches through the rather subdued streets of Vienna, after the German take-over of Austria, 13 March 1938

111

113 German and Austrian Nazis force Viennese Jews to scrub the pavements. Austrian excesses against the Jews exceeded anything that had so far taken place in Germany
114 Soon after the incorporation of Austria into the Reich, recruits were mustered for a new Austrian SS regiment to be called 'Der Führer'. Here recruits undergo their medical in the gilded halls of the Rothschild Palace in Vienna
115 Hitler did not arrive in Vienna until 14 March, as Himmler and Heydrich needed time to arrange his security. Within a few weeks the number of Viennese held in protective custody had risen to 79,000. Here Himmler and Heydrich, wearing field-grey uniform for the first time, leave the Hotel Metropole in Vienna

112

113

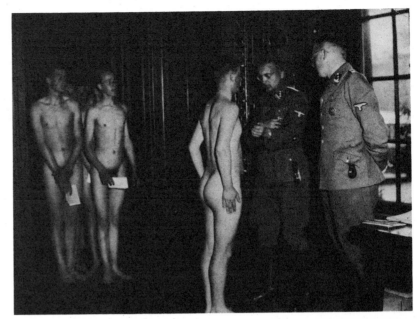

114

115

SPORT

The SS placed enormous emphasis on sport; an SS candidate was expected to win both the SA Military, and Reich Sports Badges during his first year. Later proposals that not only an SS man but also his intended bride should both possess the Reich Sports Badge was never implemented

116 The SS motorcycle team of (L to R) Zimmermann, Mundhenke, Patina, and Knees won the International Six Day Trial at Donnington in England, on 11 July 1938. When the green leather-clad and SS-emblazoned team marched up to receive the Adolf Hühnlein Trophy and gave the Hitler salute, a loud raspberry was heard from the direction of the British team
117 Heydrich congratulates SS participant Scherer who came second in the eighteen kilometre event on 25 February 1938
118 The SD team at the International Sabre Competition in Berlin included (L to R) Dr Frass von Friedenfeldt, Hainke, Heydrich, Liebscher, and Losert, Berlin 1938
119 A show jumping event at the Main SS Riding School near Munich Riem (now the site of Munich's airport)

116

119

117

118

PARTY DAY OF HONOUR

120 At Nuremberg Dr Hans Frank speaks of the new laws passed during the last year, notably that which incorporated Austria in the Greater German Reich. SS men symbolically perform their original role of protecting the speaker, 11 September 1938

121 Dr Goebbels played host to British Prime Minister Sir Neville Chamberlain at the 1938 Party Congress. Chamberlain who disliked Germans in general found Goebbels a 'vulgar common little mind', 12 September 1938

122

122 Highlight of the Congress was the consecration of new colours and standards. Hitler would hold them in one hand while his other clasped the cloth of the bullet-riddled 'Blutfahne', which had allegedly been drenched in the gore of the Nazi martyrs killed during the 1923 Putsch. As Gerd Schuman says, 'he acted as a priestly medium transmitting the magical essence of the old sacred symbol through his body to the new ones'

123 The opening of the Congress was heralded by a parade through the ancient streets of Nuremberg. Here many senior SS leaders — whose names were later to become notorious in occupied Europe — wait for the march-past; L to R: (front row) Weitzel, von dem Bach, Rediess, Ribbentrop, Moder and, in third row in cap, press chief Otto Dietrich

121

123

MUNICH

124 Hitler emerges from the Führerhaus under the fluttering Union Jack.
At the four-power conference Britain
and France confronted Germany and
Italy and to all intents and purpose
handed Czechoslovakia to the
Germans. L to R: Wolff, Scaub, Hitler,
and Martin Bormann, Munich,
29 September 1938
125 Neville Chamberlain arrives at
Munich for the four-power conference.
The difference in character between
this mild, conservative British
gentleman, and the blustering
German chancellor was summed up in
the contemporary joke 'what is the
difference between Chamberlain and
Hitler? One takes a weekend in the
country while the other takes a
country in a weekend'. L to R: Ritter
von Epp, Chamberlain, Dörnberg,
Ribbentrop and SS-Obergruppenführer Freiherr von Eberstein, Police
President of Munich
126 SS Death's Head units were
moved into the Sudetenland to
reinforce the frontier guards and
provide the cadre for the Sudeten Free
Corps, whose overt task was the
protection of the German minority,
and covert the maintenance of
disturbances and clashes with the
Czechs, Haslau, 27 September 1938
127 SS troops man barricades round
the German enclave of Liebenstein,
30 September 1938

125

124

126

127

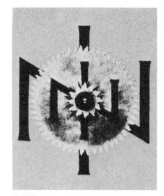

128

129

130

131

132

SALT OF THE EARTH

128 The badge of kinship which could be worn by the kith and kin of a person accepted into the SS order
129 An SS christening ceremony within the aegis of the 33rd SS Foot Regiment (Darmstadt)
130 In the entrance hall of Darré's headquarters hung a tapestry with the following fitting legend: No people lives longer than the documents of its culture! Ironically this 'document' still survives in an American collection
In December 1931 the SS introduced its marriage laws to which an SS man was bound by oath. He and his intended bride had to prove Aryan ancestry back to 1800 (1750 for leaders), submit to a medical examination and provide photographs

133

134

of themselves in bathing costumes. It is said that sometimes Himmler would gaze for hours at these, trying to detect traces of racial impurity.

The SS then attempted to replace the Christian rites of christening, marriage, and death, by neo-pagan ones. Christmas was celebrated on the 21 December and called Julfest. Marriages no longer took place in churches but in the open under a lime tree, or in an SS building decorated with life runes, sunflowers, and fir twigs (129 & 131). An eternal flame burned in an urn in front of which the couple exchanged rings and received the official SS gift of bread and salt (symbols of the earth's fruitfulness and purity)

At the christening the child was wrapped in a shawl of undyed wool embroidered with oak leaves, runes, and swastikas. Both parents placed their hands on the child's head and pronounced names like Siegfried or Wolfgang. The official SS gift for the first child was a blue silk shawl, and silver beaker and spoon. For every fourth child the mother received a silver candlestick with the legend 'you are only a link in the clan's endless chain'

Having married, the SS couple was expected to produce at least four children, but in fact the SS birthrate remained average for the country as a whole. In an attempt to encourage SS families to have more children the SS established the 'Well of Life Foundation' (*Lebensborn e.V.*). Senior SS leaders were expected to make financial contributions so that the organisation could provide maternity homes in which both married and unmarried mothers of SS children could be admitted free of charge. Despite salacious rumours about SS stud farms, only a small percentage of children born in peacetime were illegitimate

131 An altar laid out in an SS barracks in readiness for an SS wedding ceremony. Note the colours of the bridegroom's battalion, the Julleuchter on the altar, and the sun wheel emblem in the centre of the wall hanging

132 The wooden bread dish presented by Himmler bore the carved legend 'Be worthy of the bread of your own soil, then your kin will live for ever'

133 The purpose of all this selective breeding was to produce blond and blue-eyed Germans, like this proud father and his daughter. But most Germans continued to remain tall like Goebbels, slim like Göring, and blond like Hitler, Berlin, 20 April 1939

134 The Lebensborn home at Steinhöring in upper Bavaria, 1936

85

135 On 1 October 1938 Germany occupied the Sudetenland and Hitler lunches in the open with his military and political leaders near Eger, 3 October 1938. L to R: Dr Morrell, Wolff, Guderian, Himmler, von Reichenau, Hitler, Henlein, Keitel, and on the left facing Hitler, press chief Otto Dietrich

136 In the market place at Jägerndorf
a little girl is allowed by a member of
the Escort Commando to hand Hitler
a bouquet, 8 October 1938

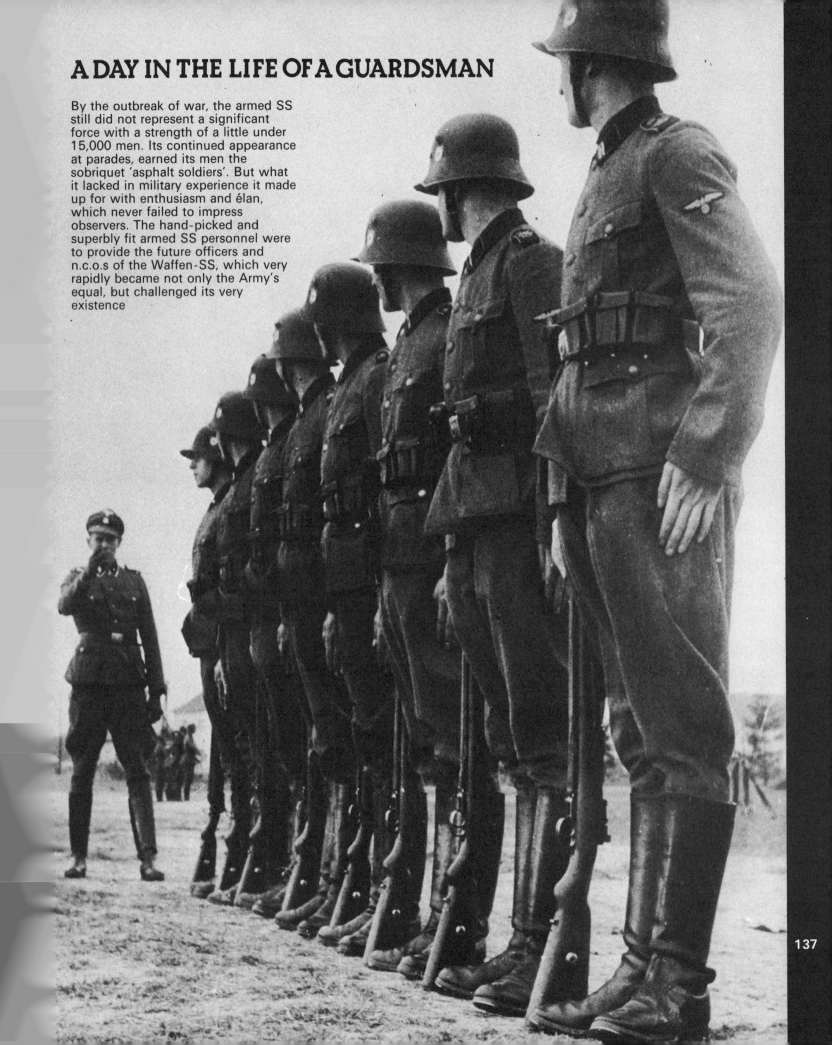

A DAY IN THE LIFE OF A GUARDSMAN

By the outbreak of war, the armed SS still did not represent a significant force with a strength of a little under 15,000 men. Its continued appearance at parades, earned its men the sobriquet 'asphalt soldiers'. But what it lacked in military experience it made up for with enthusiasm and élan, which never failed to impress observers. The hand-picked and superbly fit armed SS personnel were to provide the future officers and n.c.o.s of the Waffen-SS, which very rapidly became not only the Army's equal, but challenged its very existence

138

139

137 Although emphasis on sport and field-exercises had reduced the amount of time spent on the drill square, the SS recruit still had to learn to drill and march with precision

138 Hitler's guardsmen had five basic uniforms. The best black one was reserved for parades and leave, and the second one for sentry duty. The field-grey cloth uniform was worn in the field in the winter, while a lightweight grey one was used in the summer. Finally for work in and around the barracks he had the fatigue uniform, which he wears in this photo, November 1938

139 In the classroom guardsmen had to sit up straight with their hands on the table, but it was reported that there was a marked lack of interest in ideological subjects, and that racial policy instruction made little impact on the men

140 During the short spells of free time that occurred during a hectic and energetic day, soldiers would gather round to practise their marching songs, or sing their favourite tunes. Generally the atmosphere was more relaxed than in the Army, and the relationship between officers and men less formal

141

THE FELDHERRNHALLE

The 9 November anniversary
celebrations have been described as a
'uniquely holy occasion on which the
venerated cadre of the survivors of the
Munich Putsch silently re-enacted
their march through the crowd-lined
streets of the Bavarian capital in a
bombastic travesty of the Passion
Play'

141 Julius Streicher and the Blood
Flag head the procession to the
Feldherrnhalle

142 In the Königsplatz survivors of the
original Putsch as well as representa-
tives of the Armed Forces, followed
by a solid phalanx of recipients of the
'Blood Order' pass in front of the

massed standards of the National
Socialist formations. In the background
can be seen the Führerhaus, and the
colonnaded 'Temple of Honour' in
which the sixteen martyrs were
interred

143 The finale was the torchlit
oath-taking ceremony for candidates
of the SS-Verfügungstruppe in front
of the Feldherrnhalle, and the sixteen
smoking obelisks each of which
bore the name of one of the first
killed National Socialists

144 During the ceremony a voice
intoned the sixteen names, and after
each one a thousand voices chanted
'Hier' (present)

142

143

144

145 The assassination of the German diplomat Ernst von Rath by the Jew Grynspan was the excuse for a 'spontaneous' anti-Jewish demonstration. The resulting pogrom known as the Crystal Night caused so much damage to property that some Nazis were anxious about its effect on the economy. This photograph shows one of Berlin's newest synagogues in flames, Prinzregentenstrasse, Berlin, 10 November 1938

146

146 In January 1939 the leader of the Italian Race Political office Professor Landra visited Sachsenhausen concentration camp, in which some of the Jews rounded up after the Crystal Night were incarcerated
147 On 12 January 1939 the SS leadership paid their respects to Göring on his forty-sixth birthday. L to R: Heissmeyer, Daluege, Himmler, Heydrich, Nebe, Wolff, Best, Darré, Backe and Greifelt

1939

147

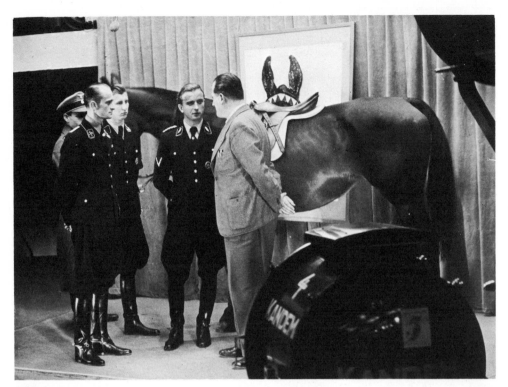

148 On 12 January 1939 members of the SS show jumping team, Temme, Waldemar and Hermann Fegelein were interviewed on German television with their horse 'Firster'

149 The finale of the 1939 Winter Relief Action was a huge 'one-dish meal' (*Eintopf*) held in the Court of Honour of the New Chancellery. Over 1,400 junior members of the Political Leaders Corps, as well as winter relief workers were served with soup by members of the Leibstandarte, 12 February 1939

150 At 6 am on 15 March 1939 German troops poured into Bohemia and Moravia unresisted. Later that morning Sudeten Germans, watched by SS reservists and customs men, removed the Czech frontier posts

148   149

151

152

151 Hitler sped through the streets of Brunn and on to Prague where he spent the night in the Hradschin castle, ancient seat of the kings of Bohemia, overlooking the river Moldau
152 The Hradschin with SS sentries
153 Peace is running out for these young SS subalterns, newly commissioned and fresh from cadet school: not for long will they be able to stroll down the Kurfürstendamm resplendent in their black uniforms

153

154 On 20 May 1939 the fledgling SS-Verfügungstruppe took part in very tough battle-readiness manoeuvres in which live ammunition was used. Hitler, photographed here with Himmler and Hausser, was impressed, and the Army had to up-date their assessment of the party army
155 In the evening of 20 April 1939 Hitler received newly commissioned SS officer cadets in the mosaic hall of the Reich Chancellery

154

155

97

156 On 24 May 1939 Hitler attended the funeral of Friedrich Graf von der Schulenburg, former Prussian general, and one of the most illustrious names to have honorary SS rank

157 The chief of Hitler's Chancellery was also an honorary SS general. Dr Heinrich Lammers is photographed here with his family on his sixtieth birthday, 27 May 1939. In April 1949 he was tried at Nuremberg for his part in drafting anti-Jewish decrees and sentenced to twenty years' imprisonment. He was released in 1951, and died in 1962

In October 1938 it was Poland's turn. Hitler began to agitate for the return of the Free City of Danzig to the Reich. Poland refused and England and France threatened to go to war if Germany invaded Poland

158 The two leading Danzig Nazis were the Gauleiter Albert Förster (right) and SS-Brigadeführer Greiser (352), seen here outside the Artushof after delivery of one of their belligerent speeches in which they exposed Polish attempts to blockade the city, 11 August 1939

159 In 1934 the SS started its own newspaper called 'The Black Corps'. It was Heydrich's idea, as he thought it would be a useful source of information. Under the editorship of Gunther d'Alquen (centre), and with Heydrich's protection, it took an independent line and was one of the only papers free from the heavy handed censorship of Goebbels' Propaganda Ministry, 6 June 1939

156

157

158

159

160

162

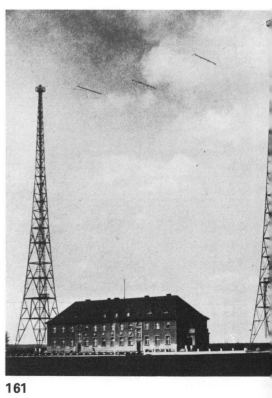

161

WAR

160 The outbreak of war on
1 September 1939 was the beginning of
the end of the Allgemeine-SS, since a
large part of its membership was
called up for service in the armed
forces. It is ironical that more of the
hand-picked and politically indoctrinated pre-war SS men served in the
German Armed Forces than ever
served in the Waffen-SS, and the
Waffen-SS was obliged to recruit
elderly policemen and ethnic Germans
from abroad to fill up its ranks.
Here an Allgemeine-SS man takes
leave of his family, September 1939

163

161 On 31 August the *Reichssender*
Gleiwitz near the Polish border was
raided by Gestapo men dressed in
Polish uniforms. Hitler used the
evidence of dead Polish soldiers
(actually concentration camp inmates
specially killed and dressed in Polish
uniforms) on Reich territory as an
excuse for invading Poland
162 Units of the SS-Verfügungstruppe
advance into Polish territory,
September 1939
163 Following closely behind the
advancing army came Heydrich's
Einsatzgruppen. These highly-mobile
commandos were to clear the occupied
territories of 'subversives' such as
gypsies, Jews, and intellectuals, and
secure important buildings and
documents from destruction
164 At the conclusion of the campaign
Himmler visited his victorious units, and
conversed with 'Sepp' Dietrich, whose
Leibstandarte formed part of General
von Reichenau's 10th Army, which
despite the rapid victory, had seen
some very fierce and costly fighting,
Guzov, Poland, September 1939

165 In this staged photograph security police officials question a Jewish woman about the banknotes concealed in her shoes

Even before Poland had been completely defeated a dark age descended on her people. Euphemistically called 'housecleaning' the German civil administration was to ensure that Poland was not rebuilt, a state of disorder was to be maintained, and a low standard of living encouraged. To ensure this state of affairs, the Polish nobility, intelligentsia, clergy, Jews and gypsies were to be eliminated.

166

167–170

166 A Security police *razzia* in the streets of Warsaw, October 1939
167–170 A summary execution by security police firing squad. After the war it was estimated that somewhere in the region of 6,000,000 civilians died as a result of the German occupation

Poland was divided into the General Government, which was to become in reality a Polish reservation, and the rest of the country known as the Incorporated Regions, which were to be joined to the Reich. One and a half million Poles were then deported from the incorporated areas into the General Government, and scattered racial German communities were re-settled in the Incorporated Regions, whether they wanted to be or not

1940

The SS contribution to the victory in the West was not so much in quantity (with only three and a half divisions compared with the army's hundred and forty) but in quality. The motorised units of the young SS were determined to prove themselves, and rushed through Holland, Belgium and France is a display of recklessness which could hardly fail to draw attention to themselves. Casualties were of course proportionately higher than in other units, but to quote Hitler, 'troops like the SS have to pay the butcher's bill more heavily than anyone else'

173 After a seventy-mile dash across Holland, the Leibstandarte drive in victory through the streets of Amsterdam en route for the battle of France, May 1940

174 The assault troop tactics which the SS had developed played an important part in the defeat of the hidebound and cumbersome French Army. Here SS infantrymen attack a defended farm, June 1940

175 The first Waffen-SS atrocity in the west was the murder by Fritz Knöchlein's men (3rd coy, II Bn., 2nd Death's Head Regiment) of about 100 survivors of the 2nd Battalion Royal Norfolk Regiment, who surrendered at Le Paradis in north western France after inflicting heavy casualties on the attacking SS. Knöchlein was tried by the British and hanged in January 1949

171 Throughout the winter of 1939 and 1940 35,000 Germans from Wolhynia were evacuated from Soviet territory. Here the Governor General Seyss Inquart and officials of the 'Volksdeutsche Mittelstelle' (right, the head of the resettlement commando Hoffmeyer) inspect a trainload of settler's wagons and possessions at Hrubieszow, 26 January 1940

172 After the entry of Italy into the war the famous motor racing event Mille Miglia was replaced by Gran Premio di Brescia, which on the 28 April 1940 was won by the SS driver von Manstein in a BMW 328 coupé

173

171

172

174

176 The man responsible for the military command of the armed SS, which from June 1940, became officially known as the Waffen-SS, was SS-Gruppenführer und Generalleutnant der Waffen-SS Hans Jüttner

177 Hitler and his headquarters staff at the end of the French campaign. L to R: Brückner, unidentified, Dr Dietrich, Dr Brandt, Keitel, Bodenschatz, unidentified, Hitler with Hewel behind, von Treskow, Schaub looking over Jodl, Wünsche,

Wolff, Bormann, Dr Morrell, von Below, Pfeiffer and Heinrich Hoffmann. Noticeable by his absence is Himmler who was suffering from stomach cramps, France, June 1940

178 The first German unit to cross the International Bridge at Hendaye on the

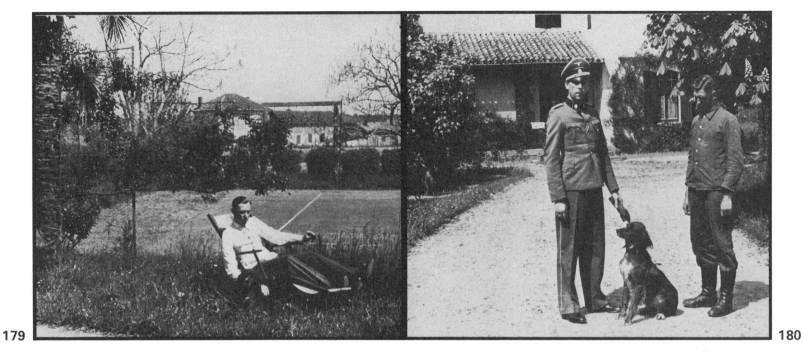

179

180

Franco-Spanish frontier was the Reconnaissance Battalion of the SS-Verfügungstruppe, 9 July 1940
179–180 After the victory in France there was a short respite in which the spoils of war could be enjoyed at leisure. Here SS-Obersturmführer

Plöw of the 2nd Death's Head Regiment relaxes in the garden of his requisitioned quarters on the French Atlantic coast, July 1940
181 The Leibstandarte-SS 'Adolf Hitler' took part in the Berlin victory parade on 19 July 1940. For the first

time the achievements of the Waffen-SS was brought to the attention of the public at large, but what they were not told was that SS dash and élan had resulted in disproportionately high casualties

181

182 SS troops practise for the invasion of England on the Dutch coast in October 1940

183 During the summer of 1940 the peacetime concentration camp guard units were mobilised, and replaced by elderly SS reservists, Sachsenhausen 1940

184 Himmler shows the Spanish Interior Minister Serrano Suñer the handwriting department of the Reich Criminal Police Office. L to R: Himmler, Nebe, Suñer, Wolff, and Reinhard Heydrich, Berlin 1940

185 In October Himmler visited Spain to discuss various questions including those arising out of the shared frontier between the two countries. L to R: Wolff, Himmler, Moscardó, Franco and Serrano Suñer, Madrid, 25 October 1940

184

185

THE FINAL TREK

The resettlement treaty between Germany and the Soviet Union in regard to ethnic Germans living in Soviet annexed Bessarabia and northern Bukovina had to be completed by November 1940. Throughout October some 45,000 settlers made the long and so-called 'final trek' to reception camps in Pomerania, eastern Prussia and Warthegau before leaving

for permanent settlement in the incorporated Polish territory

186 Types of ethnic Germans from Bessarabia. Despite identity tags many families became separated.
187 Each family was limited to 50 kilograms of personal possessions or two wagon loads. On arrival at the reception camp at Galatz, settlers were screened and processed before proceeding by train

188 SS-Standartenführer Hoffmeyer greets the Rumanian governor of Galatz Goma. In the background a river-boat full of settlers, Galatz, 19 October 1940

189 In 1940 Hitler celebrated Christmas with his Leibstandarte in their quarters in the fortress of Metz. On Hitler's right Sepp Dietrich, and behind him Max Wünsche

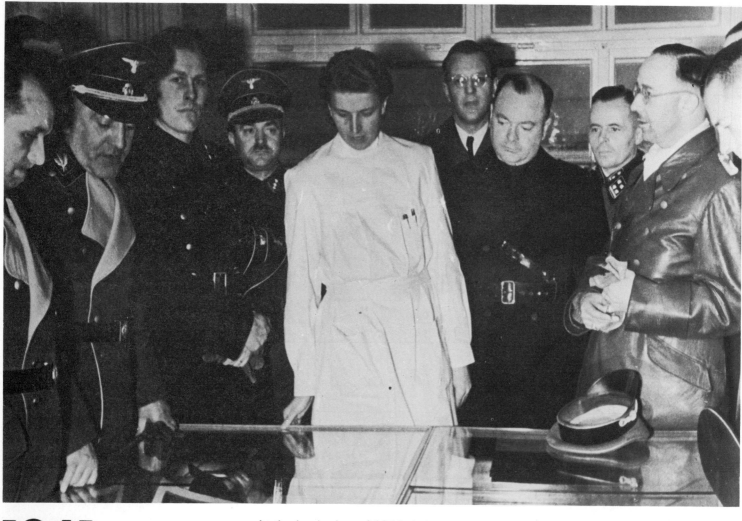

19

1941

At the beginning of 1941 there were eight main concentration camps controlled by an inspectorate and guarded by twenty-five companies of guards. For administrative reasons it became necessary in April 1941 to establish which elements of the SS were to be classified as forming part of the Waffen-SS. Unknown to the Waffen-SS proper the concentration camp system was included, and its members were to wear Waffen-SS uniform, and receive Waffen-SS paybooks. After the war when the Waffen-SS tried to disassociate itself from the camps, it claimed that it never knew of the existence of this order, and if it had it would have not accepted it.

The following set of photographs was taken in Sachsenhausen camp in February 1941, and although intended to show the German people the 'positive' aspects of life inside one of Himmler's dreaded camps, they are a unique record of life inside a concentration camp at the height of their existence. From the invasion of the Soviet Union on, the story became

one of ever increasing hardship, and deprivation, which ended four years later with the revelation to the shocked world of the most unspeakable conditions ever witnessed

190 In February 1941 the leader of the Dutch National Socialist Movement Anton Mussert was the guest of Himmler in Munich. Here he visits the laboratory of the experimental herb garden in Dachau concentration camp. L to R: chief of the Economic and Administrative Office Oswald Pohl (in peaked cap), Seyss Inquart behind Mussert, Höss, and Himmler

191 The perimeter of Sachsenhausen camp consisted of a barbed wire topped wall, and electrified fence, while the area between was patrolled by guards with dogs. In contrast to the prisoners the dogs were well housed and fed, and the chance to work in the kennels meant that a prisoner could 'organise' a few portions of dog food for himself

112

191

Es gibt einen Weg zur Freiheit
Seine Meilensteine heissen:
Gehorsam, Fleiss, Ehrlichkeit,
Ordnung, Sauberkeit, Nüchternheit,
Wahrhaftigkeit, Opfersinn und
Liebe zum Vaterlande!

192 The camp motto was prominently displayed at the camp entrance, and was painted on the sides of the huts around the parade ground (193). It read 'There is one road to freedom; its milestones are: obedience, assiduity, honesty, order, cleanliness, sobriety, truthfulness, self-sacrifice and love of the Fatherland'

193 The morning roll call took place at 06.00 or 06.30 am and lasted forty-five minutes. The figures in front of the blocks of prisoners, were the 'Kapos' or senior prisoners who usually wore the green badge of the German criminal, and were responsible for the smooth internal running of their block

194 The Rapportführer (left) reports to the leader of the protective custody camp. It usually went like this '12,476 prisoners on parade for roll-call; five prisoners died'. In front of SS officers prisoners always removed their caps

194

195 At intervals along the perimeter of the protective custody camp were watch-towers equipped with machine guns and search-lights, but despite the seemingly impregnable security escapes did occur

196 The wrought-iron slogan 'Freedom through Work' on the gates was the same at all camps
197 Prisoners clear snow in front of the gatehouse leading into the protective camp
198 The officer in charge of the protective custody camp (Schutzhaft-lagerführer) rewards deserving prisoners with a pack of cigarettes. Note the prisoner's winter clothing and ear muffs
199 The most skilful prisoner required at least ten minutes to make his bed in the regulation manner. The paliasse had to be completely level and form a perfect triangle with well-creased folds. The blue and white checked sheet had to be placed so that the squares were perfectly aligned both horizontally and vertically. Some were so afraid of being punished that they preferred to sleep on the floor rather than untidy their beds. Beds and bedding was the same as that used by the German army

200 Food was carried from the kitchen to the barrack in a special container and usually arrived cold. If the soup was not stirred the nutritional elements remained at the bottom for the server, usually a member of the camp hierarchy, while the rest received a thin watery substance. Bread was baked in camp bakeries. The bowls and spoons were same as those issued to SS troops (49)

201 On arrival each prisoner underwent the 'Aufnahme' when photographs were taken and the prisoners identity checked against the Gestapo file, and entered in the camp records

198

200

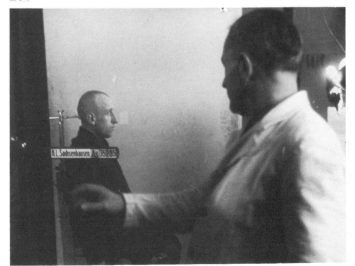

199

201

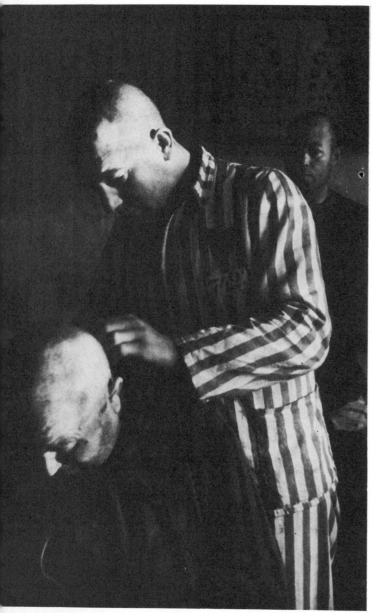

202

204

202 Even the haircut was a painful operation owing to the prisoner barber's lack of skill, and speed in which head and body had to be shaved.

203 In the prison hospital a prisoner orderly (probably a doctor in civilian life) carries out an inspection under the watchful eyes of an SS doctor

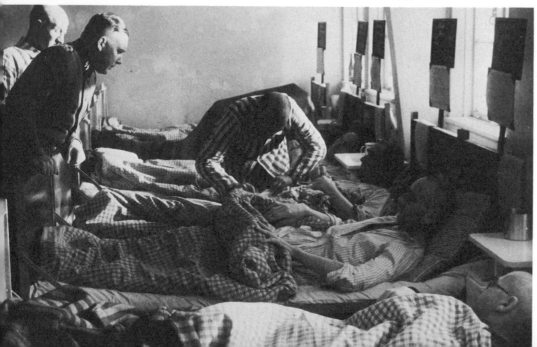

203

204 On 6 March 1941 Himmler visited the Austrian camp at Mauthausen in which the 'scum of mankind were exploited for the good of the great folk community by breaking stones and baking bricks so that the Führer can erect his grand buildings'. L to R: Kaltenbrunner, camp commandant Zieris, Himmler, and Eigrüber in black uniform.

205 The 'Totensteige' at Mauthausen where in heat or cold, prisoners already weakened by exploitation and undernourishment, carried stones up 148 steps, hour after hour, day after day, year after year

205

206 On 2 March 1941 5,000 ethnic Germans from Bukovina were presented with Reich citizenship by Himmler in Breslau

207 On the eve of the German invasion of Yugoslavia and Greece, Hitler assured the pro-Axis Japanese foreign minister that he could rely on Germany if ever Japan should find itself at war with America. Japan promptly signed a non-aggression pact with the Soviet Union, and prepared to destroy the Anglo-American presence in the Pacific. In this photo Berliners give Yosuke Matsuoka a tumultuous reception, 14 March 1941

206

207

208 Himmler congratulates members of the Reich Security Service who were responsible for Hitler's personal safety, at the Wolf's Lair, east Prussia, summer 1941. L to R: Rattenhuber (chief of the RSD), Himmler, Kempka (Hitler's driver), unidentified, Gesche, Schädle, and unidentified

208

209

210

OPERATION MARITA

211

209 Hungarian officers watch units of the SS Division 'Reich' as they rush through Budapest on their journey by road from Vesoul in eastern France to Temesva in south western Rumania, in preparation for the invasion of Yugoslavia, April 1941

210 A Yugoslav soldier surrenders to bemused members of the Leibstandarte, 12 April 1941

211 A self-propelled gun approaches the Klidi Pass, scene of the bloodiest battle to be fought by the SS in the campaign. Australian and New Zealand contingents of the British Expeditionary Force inflicted heavy losses on the SS at the gateway to Greece.

212 The advance guard of the Leibstandarte crosses the gulf of Corinth in requisitioned Greek fishing boats, 27 April 1941

213 'Sepp' Dietrich accepts the surrender of Greek General Tsolakoglu's Centre and Epirus Armies, while Max Wünsche looks on, 27 May 1941

213

212

214

215   **216**

BARBAROSSA

214 At 05.30 on 22 June 1941 Goebbels announces on radio the invasion of the Soviet Union. On Goebbel's left announcer Rau, and behind Goebbels (in SS uniform) Secretary of State Gutterer

215 The Reconnaissance Battalion of SS Division 'Reich' pauses on its headlong rush into Soviet territory, as German artillery pound enemy positions ahead

216 Motorcycle troops of the Leibstandarte pass burning Soviet transport as they enter Mariupol, on their way to the Sea of Azov, October 1941

217 In the Ukraine the Germans were welcomed as liberators. Here an SS soldier receives the traditional scarf of welcome from Ukrainian girls, August 1941

218 An SS n.c.o. with captured Soviet Army colours

217

218

219

220

219 On entering Taganrog the Leibstandarte found the mutilated remains of six of its men who had been killed and thrown down the well of the local NKVD headquarters. For the next three days the Leibstandarte shot some 4,000 Soviet prisoners as a reprisal. Here they plead for their lives, as their Waffen-SS captors decide their fate

220 In the Lithuanian town of Kovno local pro-German militia shot a group of Jews, and then clubbed to death those that showed any signs of life. German troops did not participate but hung about and looked on with morbid curiosity, June 1941

221

222

223

221 The fear of Communism, more than anything else, added impetus to the recruitment of foreigners into the Waffen-SS. This Dutch recruiting poster of 1941 proclaims that 'Europe has fallen in', and shows national phalanxes, led by Germany, resolutely marching against the fiendish Soviet barbarian

222 The oath-taking ceremony of the Norwegian SS was attended by Himmler, who told the assembled volunteers 'the formation of the "Norges SS" is a new and important step forward for the Germanic community. The honour of its foundation would fall upon Norway', 21 May 1941

223 Dutch volunteers paraded in Den Haag on 11 October 1941 before leaving for training in eastern Prussia. German stupidity and contempt for the nationals of countries they had defeated adversely affected recruitment, and many volunteers returned home disillusioned

224 SS-Obergruppenführer Paul Hausser commanding SS Division 'Reich' in his command vehicle during the battle for Moscow. In temperatures of minus 36° centrigrade the division came to within sixteen kilometres of the outskirts of Moscow, but on 5 December 1941 the Soviets counterattacked

225 Grenadiers supported by assault guns plod across the never ending expanses of windswept and snow-covered countryside, December 1941

226 The smile is still there but not the confidence, and the youthful face of the Waffen-SS begins to show the strain of the battle that it would never win

HANGMEN ALSO DIE

227 Hitler addresses the Reichstag on 9 February 1942. The President Göring sits behind Hitler, who is flanked by men in SS uniform. L to R: Schaub, Lammers, and Otto Dietrich
The Czechoslovakian Government in exile in Britain was taken in by Nazi propaganda, and began to believe the stories about the Czech armament industry's enormous contribution to the German war effort, and the harmonious relationship between the acting German Protector Reinhard Heydrich and the Czech people. It was decided that Heydrich should be assassinated, but the Czech resistance was not very keen. They argued that the reprisals would be terrible, and that Heydrich's successor would be even worse. But perhaps this was exactly what the Czech government wanted? British-trained Czech parachutists ambushed Heydrich's car on 27 May 1942 and severely wounded him, although he hung on for a week before dying. In the meantime the Czech people were subjected to a reign of terror that included the massacre of the inhabitants and the razing of the little town of Lidice. The parachutists were eventually cornered and killed, and the pathological Czech-hater Karl Hermann Frank stepped into Heydrich's boots
228 Heydrich receives a deputation of Czech and Moravian farmers, Prague, December 1941

229 Shortly before his assassination Heydrich visited a hospital train which was to be given to Hitler on his fifty-third birthday
At the wheel of the same car in which he was assassinated is his driver Klein
230 At 21.10 hours on the evening of the assassination attempt, Frank was ordered by Himmler's telegram to arrest 10,000 hostages from amongst the Czech intelligentsia, and to shoot one hundred of the most important that same night
231 Soon after the assassination attempt Heydrich's car still stands on the street where it came to a halt, while German Security and Criminal Police search the area for clues

229

230

```
+ BLITZ SDZ HEINRICH NR . 5745 27.5.42. 21.05/ HER =
== AN SS-GRUPPENFUEHRER FRANK PRAG ====
SOFORT VORLEGEN ====
1 GEHEIM ====
1.) MIT DER VEROEFFENTLICHUNG EINVERSTANDEN==
2.) UNTER DEN BEFOHLENEN 10.000 GEISELN SIND IN ERSTER
- LINIE DIE GESAMTE OPOSITIONELLE TSCHECHISCHE INTELIGENZ
ZU VERHAFTEN. ==
3.) VON DEN HAUPTGEGNERN, AUS DIESER TSCHECHISCHEN
INTELIGENZ, SIND HEUTE NACHT BEREITS DIE HUNDERT
WICHTIGSTENS ZU ERSCHIESSEN. ==
ICH RUFE SIE HEUTE NACHT NOCH AN. ====
GEZ: H. HIMMLER ===
```

231

232 The scene outside the Russian Orthodox church in Prague in which the parachutists hid. Here unfortunate members of the Czech Fire Brigade had to pump water into the crypt in an attempt to flush out their countrymen. Prague, 18 June 1942

233 At 3 pm 8 June 1942 Heydrich's coffin was carried into the Court of Honour of the Reich Chancellery for the state funeral. It was well known that Heydrich kept files on all the leading Nazis (even on Hitler himself) and many were relieved to see him dead. Himmler's first act after he had recovered from the shock of Heydrich's death, was to locate the key to the safe in which Heydrich kept his 'personal' files

234 Chief of the Criminal Police Arthur Nebe rushed an investigating committee to Prague, which reported back 'they are all so busy rushing round like scalded cats talking about hostages, reprisals, and operations, but no one is willing to consider the simple facts of a criminal investigation'

235 Karl Hermann Frank, former deputy leader of the Sudeten German Party, Secretary of State, and Chief of Police in Bohemia and Moravia under Heydrich, was ordered to assume the functions of Protector, and it was in his name that the actions against the Czech people were carried out. After the war he was tried by a Czech court (338) and publicly hanged near Prague on 22 May 1946

234

232

235

233

236 On the shores of the sea of Azov, the Leibstandarte held a summer fete in which the local population — or at least the prettiest girls — participated. Here SS-Obersturmführer Bremer awards the team of the winning chariot with a bottle of home made milk cocktail (*Kummis*), July 1942

237 The first year of victories on the eastern front netted so many prisoners that the Germans did not know what to do with them. Partly as a result of the 'sub-human' philosophy, and partly because the Germans could not cope, hundreds of thousands died of starvation. Here Himmler visits a prisoner-of-war camp near his headquarters in Zhitomir in the Ukraine

236

237

238 In June 1942 the badly-mauled SS Division Leibstandarte SS 'Adolf Hitler' was withdrawn from the eastern front and completely re-fitted as a panzer-grenadier division. On 29 July 1942 it passed in review up the Champs Elysées. Here vehicles of the motorcycle rifle company (re-equipped with the amphibious Volkswagen) circle the Place de la Concorde, while anti-aircraft guns stand by in case of Allied air attack

239 The Commanding General of Army Group West, von Rundstedt, takes the salute as vehicles of the infantry regiments drive past. On Rundstedt's left SS-Obergruppenführer Hausser

240 Although never announced in advance for security reasons, the parade seems to have drawn a large crowd. In this photo Rundstedt, with 'Sepp' Dietrich on his right, returns the salute of the staff of a rifle battalion

241

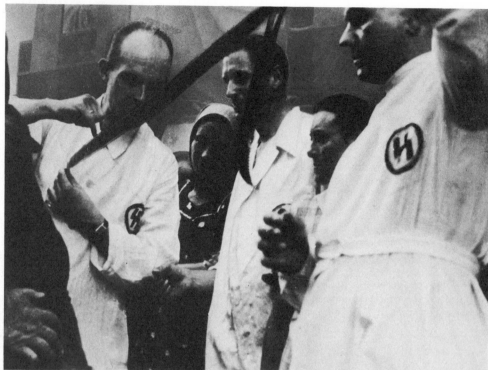

242

243

244

In October 1942 the Reich Commissariat for the Strengthening of Germandom closed all Polish orphanages, and, after medical examination, those considered worthy to be Germanised were sent to German institutions, and later to childless SS families. The fate of unsuitable children was varied, but many were sterilised.

241–242 Polish orphans wait for their medical examination, and SS officials discuss the racial characteristics revealed in the X-ray films
243 By February 1942 German losses (including Waffen-SS) numbered over a million men. Here severely disabled veterans take part in sports activities
244 By September SS Division 'Wiking' had penetrated further than any other formation into the Caucasus, and captured the oil region round Maikop. Here SS-Sturmbannführer Mühlenkamp, commander of the 5th Tank Battalion in the turret of his command tank
245 A Waffen-SS formation had fought alongside the Finnish army since June 1941, in country which froze solid in winter, and was humid and mosquito-infested in summer, November 1942

245

In November 1942 the Soviets launched their winter offensive which was ultimately to lead to the encirclement of Stalingrad. The SS Panzer Corps was rushed back to the eastern front, while other SS units fought a desperate rearguard action

246 A wounded machine-gunner is led to the rear
247 (opposite) By the end of 1942 the SS victory runes had already become firmly implanted in people's minds as the symbol of ruthless aggression, as this Soviet poster shows

246

1943

247

248

249

250

251

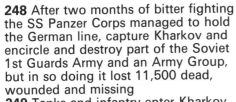

248 After two months of bitter fighting the SS Panzer Corps managed to hold the German line, capture Kharkov and encircle and destroy part of the Soviet 1st Guards Army and an Army Group, but in so doing it lost 11,500 dead, wounded and missing

249 Tanks and infantry enter Kharkov on 14 March 1943

250 These young officers, Peiper (left) and Fritz Witt bore the brunt of the fighting for the city. Witt was to become the youngest general in the German Army, and was killed in Normandy in 1944

251 The inhabitants of Kharkov and prisoners of war were immediately put to work cleaning up the mess and restoring vital services. After the war the Soviets claimed that the SS had been responsible for the deaths of 20,000 civilians

252 To commemorate the re-capture of the city of Kharkov the Red Square was renamed 'Platz der Leibstandarte', 14 March 1943

252

253 In April 1943 the Inspector of Panzer Troops visited the SS Panzer Corps' repair shops in the former tractor factory in Kharkov. Although critical of the SS during the war

Guderian contributed to its rehabilitation by writing about its exploits in glowing terms. L to R (facing camera): General Kempf, Generaloberst Guderian, and Fritz Witt (extreme right)

254 And in Berlin Goebbels received the victors of Kharkov. L to R: Jüttner, 'Panzer' Meyer, Wünsche, Kraas, Buchner, and Macher, 1 April 1943

255 Panzer-grenadiers supported by assault guns move across the endless snow-covered steppe, March 1943

256 SS-Brigadeführer von Scholz awards the Knight's Cross to the Dutch volunteer Gerardus Mooymann — the first foreign legionary to be so honoured — after he had destroyed thirteen Soviet tanks

257 An SS battle group begins to resemble Napoleon's Grande Armée. Motor transport has given way to horses and sleighs, and although the SS had fur-lined winter clothing (made in Jewish sweat shops from confiscated materials) there was never enough of it to go round, 23 March 1943

256

257

THE WARSAW GHETTO

258 'I decided to destroy the entire Jewish residential area [in the Warsaw ghetto] by setting every block on fire, including the blocks of residential buildings near the armament works. One block after the other was systematically evacuated and subsequently destroyed by fire. The Jews then emerged from their hiding places and dug-outs. In almost every case, and not infrequently the Jews stayed in the burning buildings until, because of the heat and the fear of being burned alive, they preferred to jump down from the upper stories, after having thrown mattresses and other upholstered articles into the street. With their bones broken they still tried to crawl across the street into blocks of buildings which had not yet been set on fire or were only partly in flames.' That is how Himmler described the destruction of the Warsaw Ghetto which took place between 19 April and 16 May 1943

259 Typical of the Ghetto defenders were these orthodox Jews, whose cultural and religious background had hardly equipped them to take up arms against the Waffen-SS and German police. They organised themselves into twenty platoon-sized battle groups armed with a few small arms, Polish hand grenades, and home-made Molotov cocktails. Jewish losses amounted to many thousands buried in the rubble, 57,000 taken prisoner, 22,000 were sent to various concentration camps, and between 5,000 and 6,000 escaped. German losses were sixteen dead and eighty-five wounded

261

260 'No smiles and heils for der Führer' went the original British caption to this photo of Hitler congratulating wounded servicemen. But manpower losses were no joke, and the SS was forced to lower its standards of racial and physical fitness in order to fill its depleted ranks

261 The pre-military training of the Hitler Youth was intensified by courses in special military preparatory schools or Wehrertüchtigungslager. The inspector of these camps was Hitler Youth Bannführer (colonel) Gerhard Hein who had been awarded the Knight's Cross with Oakleaves when serving in the Army. Many Germans were concerned with the ever increasing dehumanisation of the German youth, 'for whom marching exercises and bedding down in hay lofts was becoming a way of life', 1 June 1943

260

262 In the wooded mountainous regions of Yugoslavia a vicious war raged between Royalist Chetniks, Communist partisans, and the Germans. Although anti-Communist the Chetniks could not always be relied upon to be pro-German. In this photograph SS troops disarm a group of Chetniks, June 1943

263 The battle in the German rear had grown to epic proportions, as German stupidity and brutality had driven the initially friendly civilian population into the arms of the partisans. Here a mixed unit of German soldiers, Security Policemen and Russian auxiliaries is briefed before setting out in their armoured launch to patrol a river in the partisan-infested Pripet marshes, August 1943

262

263

KURSK

264 On the rolling steppe near Byelgorod between the rivers Dnieper and Psel took place the greatest tank battle of the war — the battle of Kursk. The SS Panzer Corps (4th Panzer Army) with some 340 tanks and 195 assault guns was to breach two Soviet lines of defence and cut off the 400-mile Kursk salient. From 5 to 19 July 1943 the Germans made a supreme effort, but at enormous cost the Soviets held and then counter-attacked. By then the SS Panzer Corps had been reduced to some 200 armoured vehicles. In this photograph grenadiers sit on the edge of an anti-tank ditch as the battle unfurls in the distance

265

266

265 Casualties on both sides were enormous during the battle of Kursk. Although Soviet losses will never be known, because their soldiers did not have identity discs, at least 30,000 were taken prisoner. Army Group South's casualties were also enormous, and from this date on Germany was never able to make good its losses.

266 The 'Wiking' Division war cemetery at Uspenskaya in the Ukraine. On SS graves the cross was replaced by the *Tyrrune*

267 Battered and bleeding, exhausted SS grenadiers quit the field of battle on the backs of the few remaining tanks

267

EXIT ITALY

On 11 July 1943 Mussolini was dismissed from office and arrested. Italy was in turmoil and it looked as if the whole country would fall into Allied hands. On the same day Hitler — against the advice of his generals — withdrew the Leibstandarte from the Eastern front and rushed it to Italy. He justified the weakening of the line in a vital sector by saying that 'down there I can only accomplish something with élite formations that are politically close to Fascism. If it weren't for that I could take a couple of army Panzer divisions but as it is I need a magnet to gather the people together'.

268 An SS-Obersturmbannführer of the Leibstandarte dicusses the disarming of the Italian garrison in the citadel of Parma, 19 September 1943 In August 1943 SS-Oberführer Walther Schellenberg's foreign section (VI) of the SD was told to locate where the Badoglio government was holding Mussolini captive. The task was entrusted to SS-Hauptsturmführer Skorzeny who located Mussolini in a tourist hotel in the Gran Sasso in the Abzruzzi mountains. The SD at that time had no forces at its disposal for special operations, and Skorzeny and a small SD commando joined Major Mor's men of the Luftwaffe Parachute Demonstration Battalion to gain experience in airborne operations. On 12 September 1943 Mussolini was freed without bloodshed, and as he climbed aboard the Fieseler Storch which was to fly him to Rome, Skorzeny jumped in. On arrival at Rastenberg Hitler was overjoyed by the success of the operation, and the liberation of his fellow dictator, for which Skorzeny claimed full credit. He was immediately promoted, awarded the Knight's Cross, and given a gold watch by Mussolini. Major Mors received nothing
269 Walther Schellenberg photographed after the liberation of Mussolini
270 SS-Sturmbannführer Otto Skorzeny photographed outside the Berlin Sports Palace on 3 October 1943

268

269

270

149

271

273

274

272

HIMMLER'S FOREIGN LEGIONS

In the old days it had been one of Himmler's proudest boasts that a man was not accepted in the armed SS if he had a filled tooth, but as losses grew, and competition for manpower intensified Himmler's élitism grew more realistic. Almost as soon as their countries had been occupied, the SS began to recruit 'Germanic' Danes, Norwegians, Flemings and Dutch. The first easterners to be recruited were the Balts – excluding the Lithuanians who were still considered racially unsuitable – the Ukrainians, or Galicians as the SS preferred to call them, Moslems from Bosnia, and even Indians. Having digested all these it was not too difficult to accept the ultimate in Slavs, and allow the Greater Russians to wear SS uniform

275

271 A trainload of ethnic German recruits for the SS arrive at Vienna, 5 August 1943

272 When the SS announced the raising of a Ukrainian rifle division it was swamped with volunteers, and over 85,000 turned up when only 35,000 were required. Here mounted Ukrainian peasants ride past the Governor of the Ukraine Erich Koch

273 The Latvian SS Legion marches through the streets of Riga in celebration of the 25th anniversary of the country's independence, November 1943

274 Bosnian Moslem SS men read about Islam and Jewry

275 Estonian volunteers take a rest during their training at Heidelager, October 1943

276 Himmler inspects Estonians at the Heidelager training area, October 1943
The German offensive of November 1943 on the Eastern front achieved little at tremendous cost. It culminated in the encirclement of some 50,000 troops in the Tscherkassy pocket. Hitler at first refused them permission to break out, but by February 1944, the survivors, which included the 2nd SS Panzer Division 'Das Reich' and the Belgian Assault Brigade 'Wallonie' fought their way out and linked up with the relieving forces

276

277

278

277 Reinforcements in the shape of self-propelled guns are rushed by rail from western Europe to the threatened Eastern front, spring 1944
278 Panzer grenadiers advance cautiously towards a Ukrainian village
279 Grenadiers from the Leibstandarte, newly arrived from Italy, pause on the outskirts of a typical provincial town, with its onion-domed church, and thatched *Izbas*, autumn 1943

279

1944

By January 1944 the writing on the wall must have been large enough for the many collaborators in occupied countries to think about their future in the light of almost certain defeat, and yet the most fanatical sought every opportunity to flaunt their loyalty

280 On 14 January 1944 the staff of the SS Recruiting Office in Flanders, who had been married or had children during the last year, were presented with a Julleuchter by their commanding officer SS-Hauptsturmführer Bert Schindlmayr

281 On 28 December 1943 an SS wedding took place in the Hall of Pacification in Ghent. The groom was the first Fleming to have been awarded the Iron Cross. In the background in black uniforms are members of the Flemish Germanic SS

280

281

282 Some of the lucky ones who succeeded in the breakout from the Tscherkassy pocket, February 1944

283 A sure sign of imminent German defeat was the rapid increase in partisan activity in occupied Europe. German brutality had driven many uncommitted civilians into the partisan movement, providing badly needed support and personnel. In this photograph captured Greek partisans, used as ammunition carriers, dispute with their SS captors in the Olympus mountains, December 1943
284 SS troops were hotly engaged in the fighting around the Allied bridgehead in Nettuno, between January and April 1944
285 After its encirclement in Tscherkassy the Belgian SS Assault Brigade paraded in triumph through the streets of Brussels. The enthusiasm of the crowd is indisputable, although today it is said that the Germans blocked the exits to the city centre, and prevented unwilling spectators from leaving. But this ignores the fact that after the humiliation of defeat many Belgians were proud of their son's exploits in Russia, and saw in the Brigade's success a guarantee of Germany's moderation towards Belgium as a whole
Hitler once remarked that if he had had a son he would have liked him to have been like Leon Degrelle – Rexist Leader and highly decorated commander of the Assault Brigade – seen here taking the salute

285

283

286 Degrelle's half-track draped with the Cross of Burgundy arrives in the Place de la Bourse, Brussels, 1 April 1944
287 As the Soviets drove the Germans out of Russia, SS troops found themselves encircled in Kowel in western Ukraine. These SS cavalrymen witheld every Soviet attack until finally relieved, April 1944

287

157

288

289

288 The rise of the SS from party police to fourth branch of the armed forces is apparent in this photo of the chiefs of the armed forces Keitel, Dönitz and Milch, and including the Reichsführer-SS Himmler as they congratulate Hitler on his birthday, 20 April 1944

289 When Himmler became Chief of the German Replacement Army in July 1944, he gained control of rocket development, and placed an SS general in charge of Peenemunde.

Here Himmler visits the top secret research station in April 1944. On his left General Dornberger

290 When the Allies landed in Normandy on 6 June 1944 four crack SS armoured formations were refitting in France, and were soon engaged in trying to drive the invaders back into the sea. Allied air superiority made deployment by road and rail a hazardous business. Here the Leibstandarte moves up in heavily camouflaged vehicles, 1 July 1944

290

291 In the fierce fighting for Caen there were many casualties, and prisoners taken by both sides. Here Americans wait under SS guard before moving to the rear, June 1944
292 On 31 July the Allies broke through at Avranches, and although in no condition to resist, the battered SS divisions were still dangerous opponents, 10 June 1944
293 A captured SS officer is questioned by a British intelligence officer, 26 June 1944

291

292

293

294   295

294 In July 1944 the Leibstandarte undertook the training of an ethnic German 'Pasture Protection Guard' in the Rumanian Bachka which had been formed to protect the harvest from partisans

295 Following the Bomb Plot, Himmler was made Chief of the Replacement Army. All questions relating to development and procurement of weapons and supplies, as well as all matters pertaining to manpower replacement were now placed firmly in SS hands. Here Himmler leaves the headquarters of a Waffen-SS unit, autumn 1944

296 By August 1944 the only extermination camp still operating was Auschwitz-Birkenau. The other camps in the east had either been evacuated or destroyed before falling into Soviet hands. Throughout August and September 1944 over 400,000 Hungarian Jews arrived at Auschwitz, and by the end of the war only 180,000 had survived. On 2 November 1944 with defeat staring him in the face, Himmler ordered the cessation of all further gassings. In this photograph SS-Hauptsturmführer Dr Thilo selects prisoners who are to be gassed on arrival, summer 1944

296

297 On the Western front SS men captured in camouflage uniforms were often taken for snipers whether they were or not. Some were shot out of hand, while others were beaten-up like this prisoner of the Canadians in Normandy, August 1944
298 Throughout the summer and until the advent of the muddy season, the Germans fought a stubborn rearguard action, which ended with a withdrawal across the Dnieper, but no decisive Soviet victory

297

298

WARSAW UPRISING

In August 1944 the inhabitants of Warsaw rose up against their German occupiers in the hope that, with Allied assistance, they could hand over their liberated city to the rapidly advancing Soviet Army. The last thing the Soviets wanted was an anti-Soviet national government in Warsaw, and were therefore quite content to sit on the opposite bank of the Vistula and wait while the Germans flattened both the city and insurgents. The uprising lasted until 2 October, when a Polish Home Army delegation signed the instrument of surrender at the German headquarters in Ozarow. Polish casualties including civilians have been estimated at 150,000, while the Germans lost 26,000

299 SS troops supported by assault guns fight from city block to city block
300 General Bor-Komorowski, Commander of the Home Army surrenders to the SS commander

SS-Obergruppenführer von dem Bach-Zelewski (123) at Ozarow, 2 October 1944. On this occasion von dem Bach behaved honourably and as agreed Polish insurgents were treated as prisoners of war, and not as partisans
301 Commander of the infamous Dirlewanger Brigade was the former poacher and concentration camp inmate Dr Oskar Dirlewanger. The excesses of his men proved an embarrassment to the SS, and his unit was disbanded, and Dirlewanger disappeared
302 The unit that committed by far the worst excesses during the uprising was the Kaminski Brigade, whose renegade Russian and Ukrainian personnel had a traditional antipathy for the Poles. After the rising Kaminski was charged by the SS with enriching himself and was duly executed. Here a group of 'Kamintsy' loot their way through the ruins of Warsaw

299

300

301

302

163

304

303 By the end of autumn 1944 Hungary was on the verge of signing an armistice with the Soviet Union. Skorzeny was rushed to Budapest where in another daring coup, he bundled up the pro-Soviet Nicholas Horthy (son of the Regent Admiral Horthy) in a carpet and flew him back to a German concentration camp. Admiral Horthy was then replaced by the pro-German Count Szalasi, who kept Hungary in the war on Germany's side until the end. Here Skorzeny leaves the Imperial Palace in Budapest on the successful conclusion of the coup, 16 October 1944

304 In August 1944 units of the Slovak Army aided by British and Soviet parachutists and a Czech general and his staff flown in from England rose up against the German-dominated Slovak government at Banska-Bystrica. The rebellion was eventually crushed and the President of the Slovak Government Dr Joseph Tiso showed his gratitude by decorating members of the SS security forces, 28 October 1944

305 Meanwhile in Italy the Allies were slowly advancing up the country, while Mussolini established the Northern Italian Social Republic. From the many thousands of fanatical fascists who had rallied to Mussolini, a new Republican Army, and an Italian SS Division were formed. In this photograph the Minister of Defence Marshal Graziani, and the Highest SS and Police Commander in Italy, Karl Wolff, address the Italian SS, 25 November 1944

305

306 Since his capture in 1942, the former Soviet General Andrei Vlassov had tried to convince the Germans that the only way to defeat the Soviets was by forming a Russian Army of Liberation, and proclaiming a crusade against Bolshevism. Fed up with Nazi shortsightedness and prevarication, Vlassov finally turned to the SS. Vlassov met Himmler for the first time on 16 September 1944, and although known to be unsympathetic towards Vlassov, Himmler was sufficiently impressed by the Russian to approve the formation of a Russian Army Corps. But it was too late, and the last significant action in which Vlassov's men took part, was to help the Czechs clear the SS out of Prague in May 1945

307 Hitler's final fling came in the Ardennes where on 16 December 1944 a German offensive, spearheaded once again by SS armour, attempted to split the Allies in two by striking out towards Antwerp. Nine days later and only four miles from their first objective — the river Meuse — the offensive was halted, and the Germans began to withdraw. They not only left behind the wrecks of two Panzer armies, but the bodies of 86 American soldiers massacred at Malmedy (348)

306

307

1945

308 Once again the SS Panzer divisions were withdrawn from the Eastern front; this time in a futile attempt to raise the siege of Budapest, where 50,000 men of the IXth SS Corps were encircled by the Soviets. In this photograph SS grenadiers counter-attack in the Donau region, 19 January 1945

309 The SS units in Budapest were recruited in the main from ethnic Germans, and were not considered to be all that reliable, and yet they held out until all hope of relief had passed. They then attempted to break out, but less than 1,000 reached German lines. Here a German anti-tank gun is in action on the outskirts of the city, January 1945

310 Having seen a photograph of Turkic volunteers wearing the SS runes on their collar patches, Himmler

308

309

angrily reminded his subordinates that 'only Germans or people from Germanic countries, who were worthy of being members of the SS order, could wear the SS runes. All others, who were mere mercenaries should wear some other national emblem'. Here Turkic volunteers lay out their prayer rugs

311 On the Western front the situation was no less desperate. This photograph shows typical Waffen-SS men of 1945 vintage. They are no longer the hand-picked élite of 1939, but ordinary young conscripts who were no more Nazi than the average German soldier. Flanking the prisoners Lance-Corporal John F Zuiser (left) and Private William C Mullins 50th Armoured Infantry Regiment, 6th Armoured Division, 7 January 1945

310

311

312 The commander of the encircled East Prussian fortress of Küstrin until its fall on 2 March 1945, was the former Army n.c.o. and Police General Heinz Reinefarth. He survived the war and surrendered to the Americans in May 1945 (332)

313 In March, Himmler in his new and very temporary post of Commander of Army Group Vistula, entrusted the defence of the Oder river to Otto Skorzeny. When the Allies captured the vitally important Rhine bridge at Remagen Skorzeny was ordered to try and blow it up, but in this mission he failed

314 On his last birthday Hitler inspected Hitler Youths who had been participating in the defence of Germany. Although often only armed with a bazooka they fought fanatically against Soviet tanks, and earned themselves many an Iron Cross. L to R: General Krebs, Reich Youth Leader Axmann, Hitler, and SS-Gruppen-führer Fegelein, whom Hitler was to have shot for desertion on the night of 28/29 April 1945

312

313

314

315 It was Hitler's final decision to remain in Berlin, and if need be die there. But he still continued to believe in a sudden miraculous turn of events in the eleventh hour, which would lead to victory. It was only after SS-Obergruppenführer Steiner's attempt to break the encirclement of Berlin had failed, and Wenck's offensive did not materialise, that he decided to take his own life.
In the rubble-littered streets of Berlin, a solitary knocked-out half-track of the 'Wiking' Division and its dead crew, stand witness to the fanatical defence of the capital city of the Reich, which finally fell on 2 May 1945

316 On the 18 April 1945 the American Army orders the inhabitants of Weimar to visit the liberated concentration camp at Buchenwald, to see for themselves the conditions that prevailed there. Former inmates dressed in SS uniforms were on hand to demonstrate the more grisly apparatus such as the gallows and crematoria

317 In Buchenwald hospital rows of sick and dying were found packed like sardines in indescribable filth, 11 April 1945

316

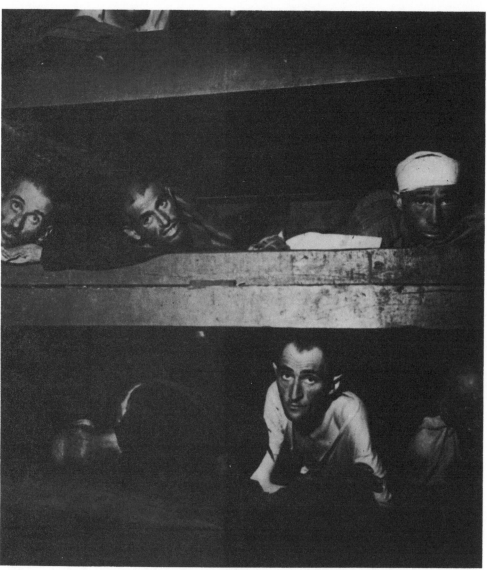

317

318 Prisoners enjoy their first breath of freedom, and lounge around the entrance to the camp compound. In contrast to those in 317, these prisoners look in reasonable condition, Buchenwald, 11 April 1945

318

319 As American reconnaissance vehicles approach a camp at Murnau in Austria, Polish prisoners rush joyfully to the wire. Suddenly a vehicle approaches from the opposite direction, and the American armoured car opens fire. Later the Americans discover they have shot up an SS staff car (**319a**)

319a

320

321

BELSEN

Belsen Concentration Camp, which the British liberated on 20 April 1945, had originally been used as a special 'privileged' transit camp for Jews with relations in Palestine, Honduras, and Paraguay, diamond workers, Jews decorated with the Iron Cross, and many others. But during late 1944 they were replaced by prisoners from camps evacuated in eastern Europe — mere disease-ridden skeletons, who were dying at the rate of two and three hundred per day from spotted typhus. In his *The Final Solution* Reitlinger writes 'it is ironical that Bergen-Belsen, after two years existence as a 'soft' camp for the privileged, should in April 1945, become the one place where the British soldier saw naked race murder face to face, the place which to British minds most symbolises the outlook and practices of Himmler and the SS'

320 SS-Obersturmführer Franz Hössler, former Commandant of the women's camp at Auschwitz-Birkenau, was photographed by British Movietone News in front of a wagonload of bodies, Belsen, April 1945. He was later to be hanged by the British

321 The Commandant of Belsen, SS-Hauptsturmführer Josef Kramer under British guard. The first adjutant of Auschwitz has been described as 'not altogether the apeman that the Allied press made him, but nevertheless a dull unimaginative brute'. Kramer was sentenced to death by the British and hanged on 13 December 1945

322 During the night of 28/29 April 1945 the Americans were only forty kilometres from Dachau, and the concentration camp guards were replaced by men from the 'Wiking' Division. It was these men who

322

324

remained at the camp when it was liberated, and on whom both the Americans and the liberated prisoners took revenge. Here members of the American press and camp officials inspect the bodies of SS men killed near tower B

323 Anybody found in SS uniform in the vicinity of Dachau camp ran the risk of being taken for a camp guard—even this young mountain troop recruit

324 General Patch's 7th U.S. Army came across another 'horror camp' at Landsberg (a subsidiary of Dachau), and photographed its commander SS-Hauptsturmführer Eichelsdörfer amongst the many unburied corpses that were found there, 2 May 1945

323

CONCLUSIONS (Cont).

61.   As a soldier and member of the Waffen SS WAGNER has still an almost blind belief in the righteousness of HITLER and HIMMLER and the justification of the Nazi ideals. He thinks that Germany failed through interference, corruption and treason among the political leaders. It is considered, however, that when confronted with evidence of Germany's war-guilt, and proof of atrocities, Subject can be converted.

62.   With no evidence at hand it has not been possible to establish WAGNER's guilt in War Crimes or atrocities. He has been cross examined on such points as the pogroms of 1938, the concentration camps etc., but without result. He and his SS division have certainly never been in WARSAW, and cannot have been implicated in the extermination of the Ghetto: in Subject's opinion this was executed by German Army units, possibly an armoured brigade. It is considered that, because of his almost constant participation in front-line operations, WAGNER has not been involved in any of the racial purges, such as were accredited to SS forces in the Eastern theatre of war. He is the type of man who would own up to his activities, however incriminating such disclosures might prove to be.

RECOMMENDATION

63.   INTERNMENT

032 Civilian Interrogation Camp,
I Corps District,
B.L.A.

6 SEP 45.

Attached Appendices A to E

325

327

On 6 May 1945 the 23rd SS Volunteer Panzer-Grenadier Division 'Nederland' – having been evacuated by sea from Courland, and having participated in the defence of the river Oder, and the bitter fighting south of Berlin – surrendered to the Americans at Tangermünde on the Elbe

325 Its commander, former Leibstandarte officer Jürgen Wagner, was later interrogated by the Americans, and then handed over to the Yugoslavs who hanged him in 1947 for atrocities he was supposed to have committed while the Dutch division was training in that country in 1943. This photograph shows the final page of the Allied interrogation summary and its conclusions
326 Jürgen Wagner surrendering his troops to the Americans on the Elbe, 6 May 1945

326

327 The 5 May 1945 issue of the Germanic SS newspaper in Norway announced, in suitably funereal tones, the death of Adolf Hitler at his command post in the Reich Chancellery in Berlin

328 The most senior SS and Police commander and Wehrmacht plenipotentiary in Italy was Karl Wolff. Since the beginning of March 1945 he had been secretly negotiating with the Allies the surrender of all Axis forces in Italy. On 2 May he capitulated thus saving many lives, but most German personnel, and particularly the SS, refused to surrender to anybody but regular troops. In this photograph an SS officer is led blindfolded behind the British lines to negotiate the surrender of his unit, which had been retreating into Austria blowing up the bridges behind it and delaying the British advance, Tarvisio, 7 May 1945

329 In their stronghold in the Hotel Regina, Wolff's deputy SS-Standartenführer Rauff calls upon his men to lay down their weapons and surrender to the American IVth Army Corps, Milan, 30 April 1945

328

329

330 The great cleansing operation had been in full swing for nearly a month in Belsen and the typhus epidemic stamped out by the sanitary efforts of three hundred British troops. On the 21 May 1945 a rifle salute was fired, the Union Jack run up, and a flame-thrower turned on the last of the vermin-ridden wooden huts

331 At 5 pm on 22 May a miserable-looking and shabbily dressed man with two rather more military-looking companions was stopped by a British bridge control detail at Bremervorde in northern Germany. The identity papers in the name of Heinrich Hizinger and the black eye patch could not conceal his true identity. Himmler revealed himself, and as a doctor made an oral inspection, he bit on a cyanide phial and was dead within seconds

332 On 25 May 1945 SS-Ober-gruppenführer Heinz Reinefarth (312), and honorary SS general and former Gauleiter of the Wartheland Arthur Greiser (158) surrendered to the Americans in Austria. Greiser was executed by the Poles in 1946, but Reinefarth was luckier (357)

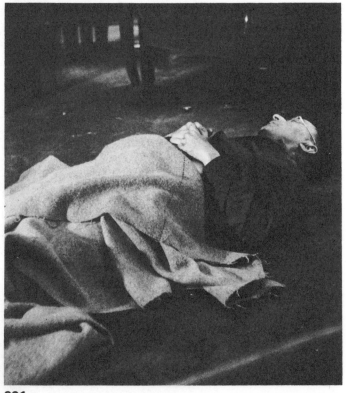

331

332

333

334

In 1945 it was difficult for Allied soldiers to understand that not everyone in the hated SS uniform was necessarily a dangerous Nazi fanatic, and that many people had donned SS uniform (not all that willingly either) as a means of liberating their home-lands from Bolshevik rule. On 2 June 1945 a trainload of Latvian Waffen-SS men arrived at Haltenklinke near Bergedorf

333 From the station they were marched five miles under armed guard to the former concentration camp at Neuengamme, where they were incarcerated in similarly awful conditions as the previous inmates

334 The prisoners form-up in the compound of Neuengamme camp. Most of the prisoners were later transported to England where many were permitted to stay. Others went on to America and Canada

335 The prisoners including this thirteen-year-old were deloused on arrival

335

336

337

336 On 24 June 1945 a great victory parade was held in Moscow. A combined regiment representing each of the fronts – Arctic, Leningrad, Baltic, Belorussian, and the four Ukrainian fronts – was led by its commanding general. The climax of the parade was the trooping of two hundred captured colours, with the standard of Adolf Hitler's Leibstandarte on the right of the first rank. The dipped colours were marched across the Red Square and then cast down upon the red marble steps of Lenin's mausoleum

337 While many members of the armed forces began to be released almost as soon as the war was over, SS men were put to work clearing up the mess. Here an unwilling SS worker, engaged on the rebuilding of the law courts in Nuremberg for the forthcoming war crimes trials, is made to stand on a block and hold bricks in his outstretched hands, 5 September 1945

338 In September 1945 Karl Hermann Frank, former deputy to Reinhard Heydrich and Secretary of State, was tried and publicly hanged in Prague on 22 May 1946 for his many crimes against the Czech people

339 Less than two months after its liberation Belsen is once again little more than the name of a place, but one which for many years to come will conjure up, not the image of a small provincial town, but a terrible place where, to quote the sign, 'people died as victims of the new German order, and as a result of Nazi culture', 4 June 1945

340 Between 17 September and 17 November 1945, a British Military Court tried forty-five former members of the staff of Belsen Concentration Camp. Fourteen were acquitted, eleven sentenced to death and executed, and nineteen sentenced to varying terms of imprisonment. Here No. 8 Herta Ehlert (fifteen years), No. 9 Irma Grese (death), and No. 10 Ilse Lotte (acquitted) were photographed on the opening day of the trial

340

341 Sixty-one year old Hermann Pister Commandant of Buchenwald Concentration Camp sits in his cell on arrival at Dachau where the Buchenwald Trial opened on 11 April 1947. He was sentenced to death and hanged

342 A number of Estonians and Latvians who had fought with the Germans sought sanctuary in Sweden at the end of the war. Despite the fact that their countries had been twice overrun by the Soviets, they were forcibly repatriated in November 1945. Many went on hunger strike and even attempted suicide, before being dragged or carried by the Swedish police onto boat or train, Eksjo, 30 November 1945

343 The inhabitants of German towns considered by the Allied occupation authorities to be unfriendly or insufficiently penitent, were forced to watch films taken in the concentration camps on liberation. The original caption to this press photograph of the inhabitants of Burgsteinfurt entering a cinema states that 'two girls who laughed during the performance were obliged to see the film again', 7 March 1946

343

344 The two most important SS men to be tried at the International Military Tribunal in Nuremberg were Ernst Kaltenbrunner (20), Heydrich's successor as Chief of the Reich Main Security Office (left), and Arthur Seyss-Inquart, former Deputy Governor of Poland and Reichs Commissar for Occupied Holland. Both were sentenced to death and hanged on 16 October 1946. In the front row are (left) Alfred Rosenberg, and in dark glasses Hans Frank, both of whom were also hanged

345

345 At Dachau the protective custody camp is still functioning, but now its inmates are some 32,000 former members of the SS. Throughout 1946 the Americans held a number of trials including those of the Dachau and Buchenwald camp staff, and the controversial Malmédy trial (348)

346 The prison at Landsberg, where Hitler was incarcerated after the failure of the Munich Putsch, was the scene of the execution of twenty-three members of the Dachau camp staff. In this photo SS man Vincenz Schöttl, found guilty of shooting a Pole who had fallen out of line to get a drink of water, stands with the noose about his neck as an American officer reads out the sentence, 29 May 1946

347 On 11 April 1947 the trial of the Buchenwald camp staff opened at Dachau. One of the main defendants was Erbprinz Josias zu Waldeck und Pyrmont (54), former SS general and the only member of a German princely house to be tried for war crimes. He was commander of the SS region in which Buchenwald was situated and was therefore held responsible for the conditions that prevailed there. He was found guilty and sentenced to life imprisonment but was released in December 1960, and died at Schaumburg in December 1967

346

348 'Sepp' Dietrich, Commander of the 6th SS Panzer Army stands trial with seventy-three of his men including (sitting in front row) the chief of staff Fritz Krämer, and Commander of the Leibstandarte Hermann Priess. On 16 July forty-three of the accused were sentenced to death, while Dietrich, Priess, and Krämer received twenty-five, eighteen and ten years' respectively for the murder of American soldiers at Malmédy. Thanks to the energetic efforts of the American prosecution counsel Major Everett, none of the controversial sentences was carried out, and by 1956 the last of the group had been released from prison, Dachau, 16 May 1946

349 The former Chief of the SS Economic and Administrative Office, SS-Obergruppenführer Oswald Pohl had avoided capture by working as a casual labourer until spring 1947. From 1942 his office had been responsible for the running of the concentration camp empire. Pohl was the principal defendant in Case No. 4 of the International Military Tribunal which ended on 3 November 1947. Pohl and four others were found guilty and sentenced to death while eleven other officials received sentences ranging from ten years to life. Pohl was not executed until 8 June 1951

347

348

349

350 One of the many Soviet war crimes tribunals was held in Berlin-Pankow in 1947, in which sixteen SS defendants were tried

351 On 17 October 1949 Ilse Koch the 'bitch of Buchenwald' was released from American captivity only to be immediately re-arrested and tried for 'incitement to murder'. She was sentenced to life imprisonment and hanged herself in her cell in September 1967

352 Case 11 in the subsequent proceedings at Nuremberg included a number of officials, some of whom held honorary SS rank. Back row L to R: Otto Dietrich (Press Chief), Gottlob Berger (Chief of the SS Main Office) received twenty-five years but was freed in 1952. Walther Schellenberg (Chief of the Foreign SD) five years and freed in December 1950. In the front row Foreign Office officials Steengracht von Moyland, Keppler (82), and Chief of the Foreign Organisation Ernst Bohle, Nuremberg, 6 January 1948

351

352

353

354

353 Four lucky members of the SS Security Service — the last prisoners of war to be held by Norway — arrive in Kiel on 2 November 1953. On the right is Dr Erwin Weinmann, former Commander of the Security Police and SD in Prague, who was later transferred to Norway, and three former members of the SD in Norway Heinrichs, Arndt, and Kerner
354 Some of the 600 prisoners of war including former members of the Waffen-SS — released by the Soviet Union — arrive in Western Germany on 22 December 1955. Their first act was to swear on oath that they had not been responsible for any crimes against humanity during the war
355 After the war former members of the Waffen-SS did not immediately qualify for ex-servicemen's benefits, and so they formed a Mutual Aid Association called H.I.A.G., which still exists today and continues to publish a monthly magazine called *Der Freiwillige*. Here an Indian looks

355

at the sign erected by the H.I.A.G. at the reception camp for released prisoners of war from the Soviet Union, Friedland, 20 December 1955

356 Hardly a year after his release from prison 'Sepp' Dietrich was re-arrested and charged with complicity in the murder of Ernst Röhm and other SA leaders. In this photograph Dietrich is taken back to the courtyard of Stadelheim prison, and points out exactly where the six SA leaders were shot, 10 May 1957

357 In 1958, the Soviet-inspired East German campaign to expose former Nazis in the West German government, drew attention to former Police General and Knight's Cross holder Dr Heinz Reinefath, who was serving as Burgermeister of the northern German holiday resort of Westerland/ Sylt. Reinefarth (332) won his Knight's Cross in 1940 as an army sergeant, and the Oak Leaves for his part in the suppression of the Warsaw Uprising in October 1944

356

357

358 Himmler's personal adjutant and former SS general Karl Wolff was living quietly as a successful public relations man in West Germany, when, during the Eichmann trial, he wrote an article on Himmler for a popular German magazine. He was then tried in July 1964 and eventually charged with organising additional rolling stock to transport Jews to extermination camps. The flimsiest of charges

resulted in a ten-year sentence, but then nobody could believe that Himmler's 'eyes and ears' could have possibly been uninvolved in the crimes of the SS

359 Wolff could not have benefited by the appearance at the opening of the Munich proceedings of former SS man Josef Faber who shouted at the top of his voice 'I am a hard core SS member'

187

360 On 9 May 1965 the Bavarian Minister of Agriculture and Forestry opened the Dachau Concentration Camp Museum, and is seen here visiting one of the reconstructed barracks. Since its opening over 3,500,000 people have visited it, and despite its obvious success it still causes resentment amongst both the inhabitants of the town of Dachau, and the former prisoners who feel that it is unfitting that the Bavarian authorities should exploit the site of so much suffering

361 One of the last major post-war German war crimes trials began in Frankfurt in December 1965, when to quote Reitlinger 'six utterly disgusting n.c.o.s from Auschwitz were sentenced to varying terms of imprisonment. But it was soon learnt that within four months the most senior defendant had been released through ill-health, and two others because of previous time spent in detention'

362 The obscure but fanatical Gestapo official Adolf Eichmann must have wondered as he paced his Israeli prison yard why, despite his lowly rank and contrary to volumes of evidence, he was being built up into one of the architects of the final solution. But then it is the manner of governments to create whipping-boys, and just as Germany singled out the Jews, so the Jews chose Eichmann, Teggart Fortress near Nazareth, 6 April 1961

360

361

COMPARATIVE RANK TABLE

Allgemeine-SS	Waffen-SS	British Army	U.S. Army
Reichsführer-SS			
Oberst-Gruppenführer	Oberst-Gruppenführer und Generaloberst der Waffen-SS	General	General of the Army (5 stars)
Obergruppenführer	Obergruppenführer under General der Waffen-SS	General	General (4 stars)
Gruppenführer	Gruppenführer und Generalleutnant der Waffen-SS	Lieutenant-General	Lieutenant-General (3 stars)
Brigadeführer	Brigadeführer und Generalmajor der Waffen-SS	Major-General	Major-General (2 stars)
Oberführer	Oberführer	Brigadier	Brigadier-General (1 star)
Standartenführer	Standartenführer	Colonel	Colonel
Obersturmbannführer	Obersturmbannführer	Lieutenant-Colonel	Lieutenant-Colonel
Sturmbannführer	Sturmbannführer	Major	Major
Hauptsturmführer	Hauptsturmführer	Captain	Captain
Obersturmführer	Obersturmführer	Lieutenant	First-Lieutenant
Untersturmführer	Untersturmführer	2nd Lieutenant	Second-Lieutenant
Sturmscharführer	Sturmscharführer	Regimental-Sergeant Major	Warrant Officer
Hauptscharführer	Hauptscharführer	Staff-Sergeant	Master-Sergeant
Oberscharführer	Oberscharführer	Sergeant	Technical-Sergeant
Scharführer	Scharführer	Lance-Sergeant	Staff-Sergeant
Unterscharführer	Unterscharführer	Corporal	Sergeant
Rottenführer	Rottenführer	Lance-Corporal	Corporal
Sturmmann	Sturmmann		
Mann	Oberschütze etc.		Private First Class
Anwärter	Schütze etc.	Private	Private

PERSONAL INDEX

PICTURE CREDITS

BIBLIOGRAPHY

ARONSON, Shlomo, *Reinhard Heydrich und die Frühgeschichte von Gestapo und SD.* Deutsche Verlags-Anstalt, Stuttgart, 1971.
BERBEN, Paul, *Dachau, The official history 1933–1945.* The Norfolk Press, London, 1975.
Damals, Erinnerungen an Grosse Tage der SS-Totenkopf-Division im Französischen Feldzug 1940. Chr. Belser Verlag, Stuttgart, 1940.
FEST, Joachim C., *Himmler Geheim Reden 1933–1945 und andere Ansprachen.* Propyläen Verlag, Berlin, 1974.
GRUNBERGER, Richard, *A Social History of the Third Reich.* Penguin Books, Harmondsworth, 1974.
HILBERG, Raul, *The Destruction of the European Jews.* Quadrangle Books, Chicago, 1961.
HOFFMANN, Peter, *Die Sicherheit des Diktators, Hitlers Leibwachen, Schutzmassnahmen, Residenzen, Hauptquartiere.* R. Piper & Co. Verlag, München, 1975.
HÖHNE, Heinz, *The Order of the Death's Head, the story of Hitler's SS.* Secker & Warburg, London, 1969.
KANIS, K., *Waffen-SS im Bild.* Plesse Verlag, Göttingen, 1957.
KOCH, H. W., *The Hitler Youth, Origins and Development 1922–1945.* Macdonald & Jane's, London, 1975.
KRAUSNICK, Helmut and others, *Anatomy of the SS State.* Collins, London, 1968.
REITLINGER, Gerald, *The Final Solution.* Sphere Books, London, 1971.
SCHECHTMAN, Joseph E., *European Population Transfers 1939–1945.* Oxford University Press, New York, 1946.
SCHELLENBERG, Walter, *The Schellenberg Memoirs, a record of the Nazi Secret Service.* André Deutsch, London, 1956.
SMITH, Bradley F., *Heinrich Himmler, A Nazi in the making 1900–1926.* Hoover Institution Press, Stanford, California, 1971.
SPEER, Albert, *Inside the Third Reich.* Weidenfeld and Nicolson, London, 1970.
SS-Kavallerie im Osten, Herausgegeben von der SS-Kavallerie-Brigade für ihre Führer und Männer. Verlag Georg Westermann, Brunswick, 1942.
STEIN, George H., *The Waffen-SS, Hitler's élite guard at war 1939–1945.* Cornell University Press, Ithaca, New York, 1966.
TREVOR-ROPER, H. R., *The Last Days of Hitler.* Pan Books Ltd., London, 1962.
WALTHER, Herbert, *Die Waffen-SS.* L. B. Ahnert Verlag, Echzell-Bisses, 1971.
'Wenn aller Brüder schweigen'. Munin Verlag G.M.B.H., Osnabrück 1973.
WERNER, Andreas, *SA und NSDAP, SA: 'Wehrverband', 'Parteitruppe' oder 'Revolutionsarmee'?* Inaugural dissertation of the Faculty of Philosophy at the Friederich-Alexander University at Erlangen, Nuremberg, 1964.
ZSCHACKEL, Friedrich, *Waffen-SS im Westen – Ein Bericht in Bildern von SS-Kriegsberichter Friederich Zschackel,* Franz Eher Nachf, G.M.B.H. Munich 1941.